TExES

Science 7-12

Practice Questions

TExES Practice Tests & Exam Review for the
Texas Examinations of Educator Standards

Mometrix

TEST PREPARATION

Dear Future Exam Success Story

First of all, **THANK YOU** for purchasing Mometrix study materials!

Second, congratulations! You are one of the few determined test-takers who are committed to doing whatever it takes to excel on your exam. **You have come to the right place.** We developed these practice tests with one goal in mind: to deliver you the best possible approximation of the questions you will see on test day.

Standardized testing is one of the biggest obstacles on your road to success, which only increases the importance of doing well in the high-pressure, high-stakes environment of test day. Your results on this test could have a significant impact on your future, and these practice tests will give you the repetitions you need to build your familiarity and confidence with the test content and format to help you achieve your full potential on test day.

Your success is our success

We would love to hear from you! If you would like to share the story of your exam success or if you have any questions or comments in regard to our products, please contact us at **800-673-8175** or **support@mometrix.com**.

Thanks again for your business and we wish you continued success!

Sincerely,
The Mometrix Test Preparation Team

TABLE OF CONTENTS

Practice Test #1

1. A motorcycle weighs twice as much as a bicycle and is moving twice as fast. Which of the following statements is true?

a. The motorcycle has four times as much kinetic energy as the bicycle.
b. The motorcycle has eight times as much kinetic energy as the bicycle.
c. The bicycle and the motorcycle have the same kinetic energy.
d. The bicycle has four times as much kinetic energy as the motorcycle.

2. Which is the best definition of an informal learning experience for learning basic science concepts?

a. A child chooses what to do, and an adult provides some intervention
b. A child chooses what to do spontaneously without adult intervention
c. A child engages in an activity which is chosen and directed by an adult
d. A child engages in a group activity assigned by the preschool teacher

3. You throw a baseball straight up near the surface of Earth and it falls back to the ground. Which statement is true about the acceleration of the baseball at the top of its path? (Ignore air resistance.)

a. The acceleration is zero.
b. The acceleration changes sign.
c. The acceleration is $-9.8\ m/s^2$.
d. The acceleration continues to increase.

4. Which part of the cell is often called the cell "powerhouse" because it provides energy for cellular functions?

a. Nucleus
b. Cell membrane
c. Mitochondria
d. Cytoplasm

5. What is a potential drawback that medical advances could have for human life?

a. Medical advances require humans to constantly re-examine their moral beliefs.
b. Medical advances have drastically increased the human life span, placing stress on the environment and the economy.
c. While medical advances have cured many diseases, new diseases may still arise and threaten lives.
d. Medical advances have given people many more opportunities for treatments and drugs depending on what they can afford.

6. Two companion models, gradualism and punctuated equilibrium, dominate evolutionary theory. Which of the following statements is most consistent with the theory of punctuated equilibrium?

a. Fossils show changes over large periods of time.
b. Fossils showing intermediate characteristics may not necessarily be found.
c. Speciation occurs gradually.
d. Evolution is a slow, steady process.

7. Which of the following general statements concerning ideal gases is true?

a. Volume is inversely proportional to kinetic energy.
b. Volume is inversely proportional to number of moles.
c. Volume is inversely proportional to temperature.
d. Volume is inversely proportional to pressure.

8. How is light created in the core of the Sun?

a. convection
b. fission reactions
c. fusion reactions
d. chemical reactions

9. Prokaryotic and eukaryotic cells are similar in having which of the following?

a. Membrane-bound organelles
b. Protein-studded DNA
c. Presence of a nucleus
d. Integral membrane proteins in the plasma membrane

10. One mole of oxygen gas and two moles of hydrogen are combined in a sealed container at STP. Which of the following statements is true?

a. The mass of hydrogen gas is greater than the mass of oxygen.
b. The volume of hydrogen is greater than the volume of oxygen.
c. The hydrogen and oxygen will react to produce two moles of water.
d. The partial pressure of hydrogen is greater than the partial pressure of oxygen.

11. A liquid is held at its freezing point and slowly allowed to solidify. Which of the following statements about this event is true?

a. During freezing, the temperature of the material decreases
b. While freezing, heat is given off by the material
c. During freezing, heat is absorbed by the material
d. During freezing, the temperature of the material increases

12. The state of matter in which atoms have the strongest bond is:

a. Plasma
b. Liquid
c. Solid
d. Gas

13. What does the energy of a photon depend on?

a. Speed
b. Mass
c. Frequency
d. Amplitude

14. In a food chain, where does energy go after the secondary consumer dies?

a. Back to the Sun
b. To the producers
c. Into the air, becoming wind
d. To decomposers

15. Which of the following planets in the solar system is the farthest away from the sun?

a. Mercury
b. Neptune
c. Jupiter
d. Saturn

16. Which of the following describes the correct short-term storage method for liquid-filled pH probes?

a. Store the pH probes in distilled water.
b. Store the pH probes on a dry shelf.
c. Store the pH probes in a potassium chloride solution.
d. Store the pH probes in hydrochloric acid.

17. Ammonia has a specific heat capacity greater than that of water. This means that:

a. Water vaporizes at a higher temperature than ammonia.
b. It takes more energy to increase the temperature of ammonia than it does to increase the temperature of water.
c. Water is always denser than ammonia.
d. Water is only denser than ammonia at higher temperatures.

18. According to Coulomb's law of electric force, which of the following statements is true?

a. The force between two charged objects is directly proportional to the square of the distance between them.
b. The force between two charged objects is inversely related to the square of the distance between them.
c. The force between two charged objects is inversely related to the distance between them.
d. The force between two charged objects is inversely related to the square root of the distance between them.

Refer to the following for questions 19–20:

A biome featuring scrubby plants and small evergreen trees has a hot, dry summer followed by a wetter winter. The following food chain exists in the biome:

$$tree \rightarrow caterpillar \rightarrow frog \rightarrow snake \rightarrow hawk \rightarrow vulture \rightarrow worm$$

19. Which biome is this?

a. Taiga
b. Coniferous forest
c. Chaparral
d. Savanna

20. What role do vultures play in the food chain?

a. Scavengers
b. Detritivores
c. Primary carnivores
d. Herbivores

21. The following is the anticodon sequence formed during translation. What is the mRNA codon sequence?

A C G U A C G C U

a. T G C A T G C G A
b. U G C T U G C G T
c. U G C A U G C G A
d. U C G A U C G C A

22. Consider the following statements about Newton's law:

I. A newton is a fundamental unit.
II. Mass and acceleration are inversely related when the force is constant.
III. Newton's first law can be derived from Newton's second law.
IV. Newton's second law can be derived from the universal law of gravity.

Which of the statements are true?

a. I, II, and III.
b. II and III only.
c. III only.
d. None of them

23. For electricity to flow and move, it requires which of these?

a. A generator and an insulator
b. A generator and a conductor
c. A conductor and an insulator
d. Electricity needs all of these

24. Lions live in savannah and grassland regions where there are tall, dry grasses. Lions must sneak up and stalk their prey. What is the most likely reason for a lion's sand colored coat?

a. It allows lions to hide within the grass.
b. The light color of their coat reflects heat from the Sun.
c. A lion's coloring helps it attract mates.
d. It allows them to run faster than their prey.

25. Which hormone is NOT secreted by the placenta throughout pregnancy?

a. Human chorionic gonadotropin (hCG)
b. Gonadotropin-releasing hormone (GnRH)
c. Estrogen
d. Progesterone

26. Which of the following statements about heat transfer is NOT true?

a. As the energy of a system changes, its thermal energy must change or work must be done.
b. Heat transfer from a warmer object to a cooler object can occur spontaneously.
c. Heat transfer can never occur from a cooler object to a warmer object.
d. If two objects reach the same temperature, energy is no longer available for work.

27. Adding a catalyst to a reaction will do which of the following?

a. Shift the reaction equilibrium towards the products
b. Increase the temperature of the reaction
c. Decrease the energy of activation for the reaction
d. Increase the purity of the reaction products

28. Which of the following statements best describes the physical structure of the universe?

a. Galaxies are the largest structures in the universe, and they are distributed evenly throughout space.
b. Superclusters are the largest structures in the universe, and they are distributed evenly throughout space.
c. Superclusters are the largest structures in the universe, and they are unevenly distributed so that large voids exist in space.
d. Filaments are the largest structures in the universe, and they surround large, bubble-like voids.

29. What is a disadvantage of using rubrics as assessment tools?

a. Learning objectives, tasks, guidance, and criteria are combined.
b. Performance levels are not as precise as grades or percentages.
c. They afford greater brevity in definition, guidance, assessment.
d. Rubrics are more concise yet offer more clarity than other tools.

30. Which of the following best describes how the water inside an organism affects its temperature?

a. Water increases body temperature by rapidly absorbing heat due to its low heat capacity.
b. Water keeps body temperature stable by absorbing large amounts of heat with only small changes in temperature due to its high specific heat capacity.
c. Water decreases body temperature by using heat energy to evaporate from the surface of the skin.
d. Water does not affect body temperature.

31. The layer of Earth's atmosphere that is closest to our planet is the:

a. Troposphere
b. Ionosphere
c. Stratosphere
d. Mesosphere

32. In humans, more than one gene contributes to the trait of hair color. What is this an example of

a. Pleiotropy
b. Polygenic inheritance
c. Codominance
d. Linkage

33. A tapeworm lives within another organism and feeds off the nutrients that are ingested by that organism. At times, this can cause the organism to experience malnutrition or death. This is an example of what type of relationship?

a. Predator/prey
b. Symbiosis
c. Parasite/host
d. Producer/consumer

34. Animals exchange gases with the environment in all of the following ways EXCEPT

a. Direct exchange through the skin
b. Exchange through gills
c. Exchange through stomata
d. Exchange through tracheae

35. Which of the following terms matches the definition: energy is conserved with every process.

a. 1st Law of Thermodynamics
b. 2nd Law of Thermodynamics
c. 3rd Law of Thermodynamics
d. 4th Law of Thermodynamics

36. Pollination involves which plant parts?

a. Xylem and petiole
b. Apical meristem and floral meristem
c. Anther and stigma
d. Root hairs and stroma

37. Which of the following statements regarding chemiosmosis in mitochondria is NOT correct?

a. ATP synthase is powered by protons flowing through membrane channels.
b. Energy from ATP is used to transport protons to the intermembrane space.
c. Energy from the electron transport chain is used to transport protons to the intermembrane space.
d. An electrical gradient and a pH gradient both exist across the inner membrane.

38. Which of the following would most likely dissolve in a nonpolar solvent?

a. $AgNO_3$
b. NH_3
c. CCl_4
d. KI

39. Which of the following habitats would provide an opportunity for secondary succession?

a. A retreating glacier
b. Burned cropland
c. A newly formed volcanic island
d. A 500-year-old forest

40. According to the kinetic theory of matter, which of the following statements is true?

a. The average kinetic energy is inversely proportional to the square of the average velocity of the particles.
b. The average kinetic energy is inversely proportional to the average velocity of the particles.
c. The average kinetic energy is directly proportional to the square of the average velocity of the particles.
d. The average kinetic energy is directly proportional to the average velocity of the particles.

41. 1 mole of water and 1 mole of argon are in a cylinder at 110 °C and 1 atm of pressure. The temperature of the cylinder is reduced to –5 °C. Which statement about the contents of the cylinder is most accurate?

a. The pressure in the cylinder is decreased, and the partial pressure of argon is less than that of water.
b. The pressure in the cylinder is about the same, and the partial pressure of water is less than that of argon.
c. The pressure in the cylinder is decreased, and the partial pressure of water is much less than that of argon.
d. The pressure in the cylinder is decreased and the partial pressure of water is the same as argon.

42. Which of the following are incorrect Lewis structures?

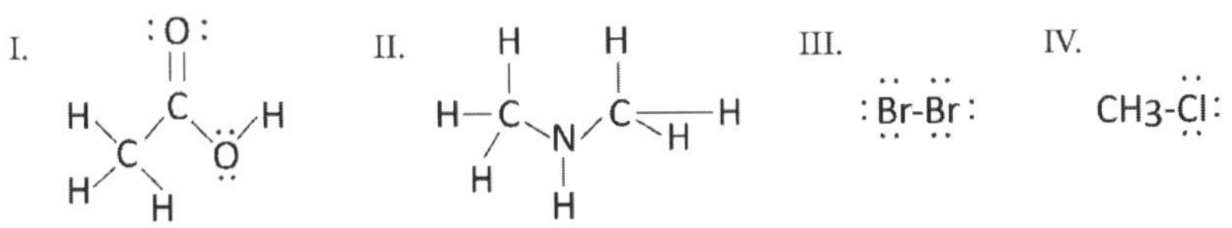

a. I and II
b. II and IV
c. I and III
d. III and IV

43. In photosynthesis, high-energy electrons move through electron transport chains to produce ATP and NADPH. Which of the following provides the energy to create high energy electrons?

a. NADH
b. $NADP^+$
c. Water
d. Light

44. The lithification process results in the formation of which of the following types of rocks?

a. Sedimentary
b. Intrusive igneous
c. Extrusive igneous
d. Metamorphic

45. Newton's First law of motion states that:

a. An object at rest tends to stay at rest unless an opposing force changes this.
b. An object stays at rest or in motion unless/until an opposing force changes it.
c. An object in motion tends to stay in motion until an opposing force changes it.
d. For every action that take place, there is an equal and opposite reaction to it.

46. All of the following are common ways of controlling eukaryotic gene expression EXCEPT:

a. Regulatory proteins
b. Nucleosome packing
c. Methylation of DNA
d. Operons

47. Four windows are washed with different cleaners. The same paper towel is used on each. The squares below show each window before being cleaned. What is the independent variable in the experiment?

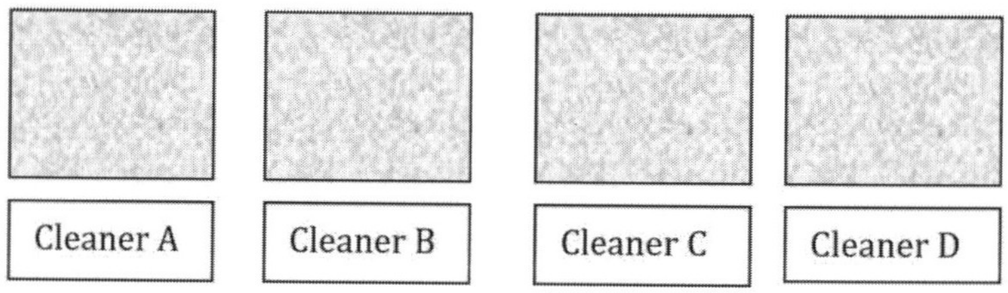

a. The amount of sunlight coming through the windows
b. The type of window cleaner used
c. The amount of dirt on each window
d. The type of paper towel used

48. A 10-kg plastic block is at rest on a flat wooden surface. The coefficient of static friction between wood and plastic is 0.6, and the coefficient of kinetic friction is 0.5. How much horizontal force is needed to start the plastic box moving?

a. 5 N
b. 49 N
c. 59 N
d. 98 N

49. When two tectonic plates are moving laterally in opposing directions, this is called a(n):

a. Transform boundary
b. Compressional boundary
c. Oppositional boundary
d. Lateral boundary

Refer to the following for question 50:

Mrs. Schubert is taking her biology class on a field trip to the local natural science museum. They have just finished a unit on world biomes, and the museum has exhibits on desert flora and fauna as well as wetland life.

50. What can she do to ensure that her students make the most of this opportunity?

a. Tell the students to pay attention during the tour.
b. Tell the students not to speak during the tour.
c. Ask the students to take notes, and tell them that the notes will be graded.
d. Give the students a pop quiz before going on the field trip.

51. Which of the following apparent colors of stars indicates the coolest temperature?

a. Orange red
b. Yellow orange
c. Yellow white
d. Blue white

52. Science has evolved as a field of study for countless years. Which of the following individuals represents the earliest contributions to the field?

a. Archimedes
b. Galileo Galilei
c. Isaac Newton
d. Shen Kuo

53. When lighting a Bunsen burner, the flame is luminous yellow. Which of the following procedures is the correct way to properly adjust this flame?

a. Decrease the air supply.
b. Increase the air supply.
c. Decrease the gas supply.
d. Increase the gas supply.

54. Which of the following is a vector quantity?

a. Distance
b. Speed
c. Velocity
d. Time

55. Which of the following is Avogadro's number?

a. 2.063×10^{23}
b. 6.023×10^{22}
c. 6.022×10^{23}
d. 2.063×10^{22}

56. Which of the following is true of different isotopes of the same element?

a. It has a different number of protons than its element.
b. It has a different number of electrons than its element.
c. It has a different charge as compared to its element.
d. It has a different number of neutrons than other isotopes of the same element.

57. Plants begin to break down the products of photosynthesis through respiration. What is the result of respiration?

a. Water
b. Oxygen and glucose
c. Carbon dioxide and sugar
d. Carbon dioxide and water

58. An inch is approximately equivalent to which of the following?

a. 25.4 mm
b. 25.4 cm
c. 2.54×10^{-4} km
d. 2.54×10^{2} m

59. Which of the following is NOT a product of respiration?

a. Carbon dioxide
b. Water
c. Glucose
d. ATP

60. Balance the following reaction between sulfuric acid and aluminum hydroxide by filling in the correct stoichiometric values for each chemical.

$$\_\,H_2SO_4 + \_\,Al(OH)_3 \rightarrow \_\,Al_2(SO_4)_3 + \_\,H_2O$$

a. 3, 2, 1, 6
b. 2, 3, 1, 3
c. 3, 3, 2, 6
d. 1, 2, 1, 4

61. Which of the following is NOT one of the five major physical properties of minerals?

a. Chemical composition
b. Hardness
c. Luster
d. Streak

62. The symbol for a calcium ion is Ca^{2+}. Which of the following statements is true concerning this ion?

a. This cation has fewer electrons than protons.
b. This anion has fewer electrons than protons.
c. This cation has more electrons than protons.
d. This anion has more electrons than protons.

63. Which of the following statements regarding the layers of the atmosphere is NOT true?

a. In the troposphere, temperature decreases as altitude increases.
b. In the mesosphere, temperature decreases as altitude increases.
c. In the stratosphere, temperature decreases as altitude increases.
d. In the thermosphere, temperature increases as altitude increases.

Refer to the following for question 64:

Guidelines for Field Journals

1. Always record the date, place, and time spent observing.
2. Describe the weather, including temperature, cloud cover, condensation, and winds, as well as any foreign (not natural) influences on the environment.

64. What else could be added to these guidelines to help the students deepen their understanding of biodiversity?

a. Always bring binoculars, since some organisms can be difficult to see with the human eye.
b. Whenever possible, sketch or describe the connections and relationships between the living organisms in the environment.
c. Be very quiet, so as not to startle any living organisms you may be observing.
d. If necessary, take pictures or videos of interesting observations for later reference.

65. A guyot is defined as:

a. Any undersea mountain more than 1,000 meters high
b. A seamount with a flattened top
c. An undersea mountain chain
d. A trough in the ocean floor

66. A 10 L cylinder contains 4 moles of oxygen, 3 moles of nitrogen and 7 moles of neon. The temperature of the cylinder is increased from 20 °C to 40 °C. Determine the partial pressure of neon in the cylinder as a percentage of the whole.

a. 50%
b. 70%
c. 90%
d. 40%

Refer to the following for question 67:

The fossilized remains of a bat have been found in volcanic rock dated to A.D. 79. Scientists studying the bat believe it to be an extinct species.

67. What would be the best way for scientists to confirm that the bat is an extinct species?

a. Compare the fossilized remains of this bat with the fossilized remains of other species killed in the eruption.
b. Search for live specimens of the fossilized species.
c. Compare the fossilized remains of this bat with bats known to be from that species.
d. Test the genetic make-up of the fossilized bat.

68. A uranium isotope is represented by the symbol $^{238}_{92}U$. How many neutrons does an atom of this isotope contain?

a. 92
b. 330
c. 238
d. 146

69. Evidence of a chemical reaction can be determined by all of the following except?

a. Modifying the arrangement of atoms
b. Endothermic and exothermic reactions
c. Equal masses of reactants and products
d. No change in energy

70. In the suburban neighborhood of Northwoods, there have been large populations of deer, and residents have complained about them eating flowers and garden plants. What would be a logical explanation for the large increase in the deer population over the last two seasons?

a. Increased quantity of food sources
b. Decreased population of a natural predator
c. Deer migration from surrounding areas
d. Increase in hunting licenses sold

71. Which of the following is NOT an environmental impact of an irrigation scheme that draws water from a river?

a. Reduction in the downstream river discharge
b. Raising of the level of the water table
c. Decreased evaporation in the area
d. Increased drainage flow

72. What is the difference between mass and weight?

a. There is no difference; they are the same.
b. Mass is the amount of matter in an object; weight is the pull of gravity on the object.
c. Mass determines the amount of volume of an object; weight does not.
d. Mass is the amount of cubic space that an object occupies. Cubic space is not related to weight.

73. In resonance, small vibrations can produce a larger standing wave that becomes stronger than the original vibrations, assuming the vibrations are at the right frequency to generate resonance. If a pendulum is vibrated at a resonance frequency, what would you expect to happen?

a. The period of the pendulum will increase.
b. The time between swings will decrease.
c. The pendulum will swing higher.
d. The length of the pendulum will decrease.

74. Isotopes are two atoms of the same element that have different ____. They have the same number of ____, but a different number of ____.

a. mass; protons; neutrons.
b. ionization number; protons; electrons.
c. charge; protons; electrons.
d. mass; protons; electrons.

75. Which of the following chemical moieties forms the backbone of DNA?

a. Nitrogenous bases
b. Glycerol
c. Amino groups
d. Pentose and phosphate

76. Which of the following sets of quantities is equivalent?

a. 2,310 mg and 2.310 g
b. 2.310 g and 231.0 mg
c. 2.310 kg and 231.0 g
d. 2.310 kg and 231,000 mg

77. You are watching the Olympic ice skating championships and see the pairs are up next. They begin their routine facing each other with their palms up and against each other. When the music starts they push themselves apart with their palms. What type of force is this?

a. Magnetic
b. Balanced
c. Action and reaction force
d. Centripetal force

78. Which statement best explains the Biological Species Concept (BSC)?

a. It states that the status of species is based on the ability to pass on the most successful traits to their offspring.
b. It states that the status of species is based on the reproductive isolation of populations.
c. It states that the status of species is based on the ability of populations to mix and produce fertile hybrids.
d. It states that the status of a species is due to the theory of natural selection.

79. Suppose your actual weight is 150 pounds and you weigh yourself with an analog scale and get a reading of 152.1 pounds. You repeat the measurement twice more and get 152.1 pounds each time. Which of the following statements is true?

a. There is no random error.
b. There is no systematic error.
c. The systematic error is 2.1 pounds.
d. The random error is 2.1 pounds.

80. A teacher provides her students with the checklist shown below for homework. What is the most likely purpose of the activity?

	Me	Parent 1	Parent 2
Eye color			
Ability to roll tongue			
Presence of widow's peak			
Hand dominance			
Presence of dimples			

a. To illustrate the purpose of taking medical history in the event of illness on a smaller, less negative scale.
b. To demonstrate how genetics plays a role in determining what traits are passed through generations.
c. To help students feel connected to parents during a tumultuous social period by identifying basic similarities.
d. To show the process of Darwin's theories of natural selection in humans.

81. Which of the following is considered observational evidence in support of the Big Bang Theory?

a. Expansion in the redshifts of galaxies
b. Measurements of cosmic microwave background radiation
c. Measurements of the distribution of quasars and galaxies
d. All of the above

82. The Punnett square shown here indicates a cross between two parents, one with alleles BB and the other with alleles Bb. Select the correct entry for the upper right box in the Punnett square, which is indicated with the letter, *x*:

	B	**B**
B		*x*
b		

a. Bb
b. bB
c. BB
d. bb

83. The specific heat capacity of ice is half as much as that of liquid water. What is the result of this?

a. It takes half the amount of energy to increase the temperature of a 1 kg sample of ice by 1 °C than a 1 kg sample of water.
b. It takes twice the amount of energy to increase the temperature of a 1 kg sample of ice by 1 °C than a 1 kg sample of water.
c. It takes a quarter the amount of energy to increase the temperature of a 1 kg sample of ice by 1 °C than a 1 kg sample of water.
d. It takes the same amount of energy to increase the temperature of a 1 kg sample of ice and a 1 kg sample of water by 1 °C.

84. Ms. Burke plans to illustrate the difference between physical and chemical changes in substances. Which experiment can the students perform that will allow the students to observe a chemical change?

a. The students place an ice cube in a bowl and allow it to melt. They can then place the dish into the freezer, causing it to re-form into another shape.
b. A variety of objects, including metal nails, are left on the windowsill outside of the classroom for a period of time. Students observe and document the changes, including rust forming on the nails.
c. Students observe and record evaporation rates of water from various kinds of receptacles.
d. A food preparation area allows students to create their own snacks. While preparing the food, students observe the spreading of cream cheese on crackers, the melting of butter onto bread, and milk being added to cereals.

85. Which of the following is true about how light interacts with matter?

a. The sky is blue because molecules in the atmosphere scatter short-wavelength (blue) light more than other colors.
b. The sky is blue because the atmosphere absorbs only blue wavelengths.
c. Glass is transparent to all of the frequencies of light within the spectrum.
d. Wood, metal, and other opaque materials reflect all wavelengths of light.

86. What type of compound is formed by the combination of two or more nonmetallic elements with one another?

a. Organic
b. Ionic
c. Covalent
d. Chemical

87. Which type of plant does NOT produce seeds?

a. Monocots
b. Angiosperms
c. Gymnosperms
d. Nonvascular plants

88. Which part of a flower collects pollen?

a. Style
b. Stigma
c. Petals
d. Sepals

89. What other planet in the solar system experiences a greenhouse effect similar to that observed on Earth?

a. Mercury
b. Venus
c. Neptune
d. Saturn

90. A total solar eclipse can be observed only by viewers located:

a. Within the penumbra but outside of the umbra
b. Within the umbra
c. Within either the umbra or the penumbra
d. Outside of the Moon's penumbra

91. Which of the following is NOT considered a layer of the heart?

a. Epicardium
b. Endocardium
c. Myocardium
d. Vasocardium

92. Which of the following assessment methods is most likely to be used in a learner-centered classroom?

a. A method that provides different alternatives for students to demonstrate their knowledge
b. A method that allows students to complete the assessment in groups
c. A structured method that allows students' mastery to be compared with that of other students
d. A multiple-choice test which students help to construct and grade

93. Which of the following describes the process skill of concluding?

a. Explaining or interpreting observations
b. Making a determination based on the results of a controlled experiment
c. Reading an instrument during an experiment
d. Listing similarities and differences between two objects

Refer to the following for questions 94–95:

The planet's oceans are experiencing climate changes, pollution, and overfishing. In some areas, zones that would normally host abundant aquatic life are now considered "dead zones."

94. Which of the following causes of ocean destruction is not a result of human activity?

a. Diminishment of coral reefs
b. Destruction of food webs
c. Increased population of all species
d. Degradation or total loss of wetlands

95. The main human-caused reason for these "dead zones" is:

a. Evaporation
b. Invasive species
c. Use of chemical fertilizers
d. Global warming

96. Which of the following statements concerning earthquakes is NOT true?

a. The epicenter is located on the Earth's surface directly above the focus.
b. Large earthquakes near or beneath a large body of water can generate deadly tsunamis.
c. The epicenter may be located by combining seismograms from two widely separate locations.
d. P waves, which travel faster than S waves, tend to have lower amplitude than S waves, causing little damage.

97. Which of the following are formed when the plasma membrane surrounds a particle outside of the cell?

a. Golgi bodies
b. Rough endoplasmic reticulum
c. Secretory vesicles
d. Endocytic vesicles

98. Semiconductors belong to what group of elements?

a. alkaline earth metals
b. halogens
c. metalloids
d. noble gases

99. Transfer of DNA between bacteria using a narrow tube called a pilus is known as:

a. Transformation
b. Transduction
c. Operation
d. Conjugation

100. You blow up a rubber balloon and hold the opening tight with your fingers. You then release your fingers, causing air to blow out of the balloon. This pushes the balloon forward, causing the balloon to shoot across the room. Which of Newton's laws best explains the cause of this motion?

a. Newton's First Law
b. Newton's Second Law
c. Newton's Third Law
d. Newton's Fourth Law

101. When materials that are attracted by magnets align at right angles to the lines of the magnetic force field, the name for this is:

a. Magnetic induction
b. Ferromagnetism
c. Paramagnetism
d. Diamagnetism

102. Which of the following best describes the primary function of carbohydrates?

a. Provide energy
b. Aid in metabolism
c. Muscle tissue function
d. Prevents cell damage

103. Which of the following plant organelles contain the pigment that gives green leaves their color?

a. Centrioles
b. Cell walls
c. Chloroplasts
d. Central vacuole

Refer to the following for question 104:

After a laboratory experiment that involved using various chemical solutions, you and your lab partner are asked to clean up your workspace. The teacher states that any chemicals that have been poured into a new container should be disposed of, but the chemicals still in their original bottles can be placed into storage.

104. Which of the following is NOT a recommended storage practice for laboratory chemicals?

a. Chemicals should be stored at the appropriate temperature and humidity.
b. Chemicals should be dated when received and when opened.
c. Chemicals may be routinely stored on bench tops.
d. Chemicals should be stored on shelves with raised outer edges.

105. In the reaction $Pb + H_2SO_4 \rightarrow PbSO_4 + H_2$

a. Lead is reduced and hydrogen is oxidized
b. Lead is oxidized and hydrogen is oxidized
c. Lead is reduced and sulfate is oxidized
d. Lead is oxidized and hydrogen is reduced

106. Which of the following plant structures allows for gas exchange?

a. Xylem
b. Phloem
c. Cuticle
d. Stomata

107. Which of the following is responsible for the passage of water through a plant?

a. Cohesion
b. Adhesion
c. Osmosis
d. Transpiration

108. The energy flow through an ecosystem is represented by an energy pyramid. In the energy pyramid for a terrestrial ecosystem, the producers utilize 6,000 kilocalories per square meter per year. What approximate amount of energy is transferred to the third trophic level of this ecosystem?

a. 0.6 kilocalories per square meter per year
b. 6 kilocalories per square meter per year
c. 60 kilocalories per square meter per year
d. 600 kilocalories per square meter per year

109. Which of the following mutations is most likely to have a dramatic effect on the sequence of a protein?

a. A point mutation
b. A missense mutation
c. A deletion
d. A silent mutation

110. A person walks 4 meters in a single direction. He or she then changes directions and walks an additional 9 meters. What is the total magnitude of the displacement of the person?

a. It is 13 meters.
b. It is always larger than 9 meters but less than 13 meters.
c. It is less than 13 meters and as small as 5 meters.
d. It is less than 5 meters.

111. Which of the following is NOT a characteristic of enzymes?

a. They change shape when they bind their substrates.
b. They can catalyze reactions in both forward and reverse directions.
c. Their activity is sensitive to changes in temperature.
d. They are always active on more than one kind of substrate.

112. Methylmercury is a toxin produced indirectly from what energy source?

a. Oil
b. Natural gas
c. Wood
d. Coal

113. Which of the following is NOT true about land reclamation?

a. Land for agricultural use may be reclaimed by draining submerged wetlands.
b. Land reclamation may destroy habitats and increase biodiversity.
c. Land reclamation creates new lands from ocean beds, riverbeds, or lakebeds.
d. Land reclamation may result in soil liquefaction during earthquakes.

114. Which of the following ideas most aligns with Darwin's work in *On the Origin of Species*?

a. If an organism changes during its life in order to adapt to its environment, those changes are passed on to its offspring.
b. The geological processes that alter the earth are uniform through time.
c. Human populations will rapidly increase unless kept in check by limits in food supply.
d. Nature selects the best-adapted varieties to survive and reproduce.

115. Which of the following subatomic particles has the smallest mass?

a. Protons
b. Electrons
c. Quarks
d. Neutrons

116. Which has a greater moment of inertia about an axis through its center: a solid cylinder or a hollow cylinder? Both cylinders have the same mass and radius.

a. Solid cylinder
b. Hollow cylinder
c. Both have the same moment of inertia.
d. It depends on how quickly the cylinders are rolling.

117. Minerals that form on the sea floor from discarded shells are most likely part of which chemical class?

a. Sulfate
b. Organic
c. Carbonate
d. Silicate

118. Which of the following statements about isotopes of an element is true?

a. They have the same number of nucleons.
b. They have the same number of neutrons, but different numbers of protons.
c. They have the same number of protons, but different numbers of neutrons.
d. They have a different number of electrons.

119. When using a microscope, which objective provides the greatest field of view?

a. 4X
b. 10X
c. 40X
d. 100X

120. Which of the following demonstrations best illustrates Newton's first law?

a. Giving a small push to a billiard ball that was at rest on a smooth, level table and letting it roll on the table
b. Dragging a box on a table at a constant speed by exerting just enough force to overcome the force of friction
c. Trying without success to move a heavy bureau or filing cabinet on the floor
d. Running a current through two parallel wires

121. Which of the following is a source of renewable energy?

a. Nuclear power
b. Natural gas
c. Geothermal power
d. Crude oil

122. The two criteria for classifying epithelial tissue are *cell layers* and ________. Which of the following completes the sentence above?

a. cell composition
b. cell absorption
c. cell shape
d. cell stratification

123. Molten magnesium chloride is electrolyzed. The products formed from this reaction are:

a. Mg at the anode and Cl^- at the cathode
b. Mg^{2+} at the anode and Cl^- at the cathode
c. Mg at the cathode and Cl_2 at the anode
d. Mg at the anode and Cl_2 at the cathode

124. A nucleus absorbs a neutron and undergoes a fission reaction. Which of the following statements explains why this happens?

a. The nucleus is more stable with the additional neutron.
b. The new nucleus is unstable.
c. Energy is released.
d. The binding energy per nucleon decreases.

125. Which action will help dissolve a gas in a liquid if the gas and liquid are placed in a sealed container?

a. Heat the liquid.
b. Cool the liquid.
c. Shake the container.
d. Decrease the pressure on the lid.

126. According to the geologic time scale, which of the following statements is NOT true?

a. The rise of human civilization occurred between 6,000 and 12,000 years ago.
b. The Cambrian explosion occurred after the Jurassic Period.
c. Amphibians appeared before reptiles, mammals, and birds.
d. Spontaneous generation of the first cells occurred approximately 4,000,000,000 years ago.

127. Which of the following would create the greatest amount of genetic variation for a diploid species in a single generation?

a. Crossing over
b. Mutation
c. Hybridization
d. Independent assortment of homologs

128. When a population reaches its carrying capacity:

a. Other populations will be forced out of the habitat.
b. Density-dependent factors no longer play a role.
c. Density-independent factors no longer play a role.
d. The population growth rate approaches zero.

129. During the *anaphase* of mitosis, the _____________, originally in pairs, separate from their daughters and move to the opposite ends (or poles) of the cell.

a. Chromosomes
b. Spindle fibers
c. Centrioles
d. Nuclear membranes

130. Which of the following household products is NOT correctly matched with the formula of the chemical it's associated with?

a. Salt, $NaCl$
b. Sugar, $C_{12}H_{22}O_{11}$
c. Hydrogen peroxide, H_2O_2
d. Chalk, $NaCO_3$

131. Which of the following is NOT generally true regarding solubility?

a. Increasing temperature increases the solubility of a solid in a liquid.
b. Increasing temperature increases the solubility of a gas in a liquid.
c. Increasing the pressure has little effect on the solubility of a solid in a liquid.
d. Increasing partial pressure of a gas increases the solubility of a gas in a liquid.

132. Which of the following is a disadvantage of fossil fuels?

a. Extraction processes are extremely dangerous.
b. There is no way to control pollution from their processing.
c. They are difficult to store safely.
d. Their use contributes to global warming.

133. Which of the following is NOT a statement of one of the laws established by Isaac Newton?

a. The lateral pressure exerted by a moving fluid decreases as the fluid's speed increases.
b. For every action there is an opposite and equal reaction.
c. The acceleration of an object is directly related to the force applied to the object and inversely related to the object's mass.
d. The attraction between two objects is directly related to the masses of the objects and inversely related to the square of the distance between the two objects.

134. Which of the following is correct regarding how objects produce sound and how we hear it?

a. Sound is something that causes vibrations in the air.
b. Sound waves are vibrations disturbing media like air.
c. Sound causes vibrations in the air but not in the ear.
d. Sound is the same energy type in the ear and brain.

135. Which of the following is NOT an example of chemical weathering of rocks?

a. Highly acidic rainwater causes dissolution of rocks.
b. Anhydrous minerals in rocks absorb water, causing them to enlarge and create fractures within the rocks.
c. Salt water penetrates fractures in rocks and leaves behind salt crystals that cause fractures.
d. Iron molecules in rocks react with atmospheric oxygen, which causes oxidation.

136. Under which conditions will light undergo total internal reflection?

a. When the angle of incidence is equal to the critical angle
b. When the angle of incidence is greater than the critical angle
c. When the angle of incidence is less than the critical angle
d. When the angle of incidence is zero

137. Magnesium metal is reacted with hydrobromic acid according to the following equation:

$$Mg + 2HBr \rightarrow MgBr_2 + H_2$$

If 100 g of Mg is reacted with 100 g of HBr, which statement about the reaction is true?

a. Mg is the limiting reagent.
b. HBr is the excess reagent.
c. Mg is the excess reagent.
d. 100 g of $MgBr_2$ will be produced.

138. The amount of potential energy an object has depends on all of the following except its

a. Mass
b. Height above ground
c. Gravitational attraction
d. Temperature

139. Which of the following is a proposed explanation for the formation of black holes?

a. High-energy collisions
b. Gravitational collapse
c. Accretion of matter
d. A and B

140. Which of the following creates an electromagnet?

a. Rapidly spinning and rotating electrons inside an iron bar
b. An iron bar moving inside a coil of wire that contains a current
c. The movement of electrons through a complete circuit
d. Convection currents within the liquid core of Earth's interior

Answer Key and Explanations for Test #1

1. B: Kinetic energy is the energy of motion and is defined as $KE = \frac{1}{2}mv^2$. Using this equation, if you double the mass and the velocity of an object, you find $KE = \frac{1}{2}(2m')(2v')^2$, or 8 times the original KE. Therefore, the motorcycle has 8 times as much kinetic energy as the bicycle.

2. A: When young children learn basic science concepts, an informal learning experience is defined as one wherein the child has choice and control over the activity, but at some point during the activity an adult provides some kind of intervention. When the child has complete choice and control of the activity and no adult intervenes at all (B), this is the definition of a naturalistic learning experience. If the child's activity is chosen and directed by an adult (C), or assigned to a group of children in preschool by the teacher (D), these are examples of structured learning experiences.

3. C: This is a problem of free fall in two dimensions. A thrown ball without air resistance will only be subjected to one force, gravity. This causes a downward acceleration of exactly $9.8\ m/s^2$ on all objects, regardless of their size, speed or position. Note: since the ball was thrown directly upwards, the horizontal acceleration is $0\ m/s^2$ and the horizontal speed at all times is $0\ m/s$. B is wrong because the force of gravity is always pointed downward and never changes direction.

4. C: Mitochondria are often called the power house of the cell because they provide energy for the cell to function. The nucleus is the control center for the cell. The cell membrane surrounds the cell and separates the cell from its environment. Cytoplasm is the thick fluid within the cell membrane that surrounds the nucleus and contains organelles.

5. B: A longer life span does not necessarily lead to more productive years. It also leads to a larger aged population and increases the rate of population growth. Re-examining moral beliefs is not necessarily a drawback. New diseases may arise but medical advances may aid in the cure of these diseases.

6. B: Gradualism states that evolution occurs slowly, with organisms exhibiting small changes over long periods of time. According to gradualism, the fossil record should show gradual changes over time. Punctuated equilibrium states that evolution occurs in spurts of sudden change. According to punctuated equilibrium, the fossil record should have large gaps.

7. D: According to Boyle's law, the volume of a gas is inversely proportional to pressure. As pressure increases, volume decreases. According to Avogadro's law, the volume of a gas is proportional to the number of moles. As the number of moles increases, volume increases. According to Charles's law, the volume of a gas is proportional to the temperature in kelvins. As the temperature increases, volume increases. Since temperature is a measure of the kinetic energy of a gas, volume is proportional to the kinetic energy.

8. C: Sunlight consists of photons and cosmic rays. Sunlight is produces when hydrogen, deuterium, and tritium nuclei combine to form helium. This nuclear reaction is called fusion. Fission occurs when a nucleus disintegrates into two smaller nuclei. In both fission and fusion, energy is released because the binding energy per nucleon increases. This decreases the mass of the nuclei.

9. D: Both prokaryotes and eukaryotes interact with the extracellular environment and use membrane-bound or membrane-associated proteins to achieve this. They both use diffusion and active transport to move materials in and out of their cells. Prokaryotes have very few proteins associated with their DNA, whereas eukaryotes' DNA is richly studded with proteins. Both types of living things can have flagella, although with different structural characteristics in the two groups. The most important differences between prokaryotes and eukaryotes are the lack of a nucleus and membrane-bound organelles in prokaryotes.

10. D: Since there are twice as many molecules of hydrogen as molecules of oxygen, the partial pressure of hydrogen will be greater. The mass of hydrogen will not be greater than the mass of oxygen present even though there are more moles of hydrogen, due to oxygen having a higher molecular weight. Each gas will occupy the same volume. Hydrogen and oxygen gas can coexist in the container without reacting to produce water. There is no indication given that a chemical reaction has occurred.

11. B: Freezing is an exothermic event; therefore, heat must be given off. The temperature of the material remains unchanged at the freezing point during the process.

12. C: The state of matter in which atoms have the strongest bond is the solid state. Matter, which is defined as any substance that has mass and occupies space, can exist as a solid, liquid, gas, or plasma. The atoms or molecules that form solids possess the strongest bonds, while those that form plasma possess the weakest bonds.

13. C: The energy of a photon is determined by $E = hf$ in which E represents the energy of a photon, h is Planck's constant, and f represents the frequency of the photon. Therefore, the energy of a photon depends on the frequency of the photon.

14. D: After a secondary consumer dies, such as a wolf, its body is partially consumed by decomposers, such as bacteria and fungi. Bacteria and fungi live in soil and digest body tissues of dead organisms, converting them into basic nutrients that plants need to grow. Therefore, after secondary consumers die, their energy is consumed by decomposers, who make nutrients available in the soil for producers to use. *Do not confuse nutrients in the soil with energy that producers get from the Sun to make their own food.*

15. B: Neptune is the farthest of the planets listed from the sun. Mercury is the closest planet in our solar system from the sun. In increasing order of distance from the sun, Venus is second; Earth is third; Mars is fourth; Jupiter is fifth; and Saturn is sixth. Since Pluto was demoted from the status of planet to dwarf planet in 2006 when technology advances permitted clearer observation of it, it is no longer considered the farthest planet from the sun as it is no longer considered a planet. This makes Neptune the farthest planet away from the sun.

16. C: The pH probes should be stored according to the manufacturer's instructions. In general, pH probes should never be stored in water or stored dry without first draining the electrode. They should always be stored in an appropriate buffer or reference electrolyte, which is usually a 3M – 4M potassium chloride solution.

17. B: The fact that water's specific heat capacity is second only to that of ammonia means that it takes more energy to increase the temperature of ammonia than it does to increase the temperature of water. Specific heat capacity refers to the amount of energy required to increase the temperature of a substance by one degree Celsius. Ammonia has the highest specific heat capacity of all substances, and the specific heat capacity of water is the second highest.

18. B: Coulomb's law of electric force is represented by $F = k\frac{q_1q_2}{d^2}$ in which F is the force of attraction, k is a constant related to the medium between the charges, q_1 and q_2 are the strengths of the charges, and d is the distance between the charges. Since the square of the distance is in the denominator, the force is inversely related to the square of the distance between the charges.

19. C: The chaparral biome features scrubby plants and small evergreen trees and also has a hot, dry summer followed by a wetter winter. This biome is mainly found around the Mediterranean Sea, though there are also chaparrals in Australia, South Africa, and the American Southwest. The taiga is a colder biome found primarily in northern Europe and Asia. The vegetation of the taiga is mainly scattered stands of coniferous trees. A coniferous forest, meanwhile, is a warmer forest composed of trees that have needles and cones rather than leaves. These trees are better suited for a cold climate than are deciduous trees. A savanna is a tropical grassland with only a few trees. Savannas are clustered around the equator.

20. A: Vultures eat carrion, or dead animals, so they are considered scavengers. Detritivores are heterotrophs that eat decomposing organic matter such as leaf litter. They are usually small.

21. C: Translation is the process of the tRNA bringing the correct amino acid to the ribosome according to the sequence of the mRNA. Since translation only involves RNA, the four bases are adenine (A), cytosine (C), guanine (G), and uracil (U). There is no thymine (T) used in RNA. Cytosine (C) and guanine (G) pair and adenine (A) and uracil (U) pair. A codon is the triplet sequence that represents a specific amino acid or a start/stop point. It is on the messenger RNA (mRNA). The anticodon is on tRNA and corresponds to the amino acid used by the ribosome during translation. They are complementary. UGC becomes AUG; AUG becomes CGA. The mRNA codon sequence is U G C A U G C G A if the anticodon sequence formed during translation is A C G U A C G C U.

22. B: The newton can be defined in terms of the fundamental units of meters, kilograms, and seconds as $\text{N} = \text{kg} \times \text{m/s}^2$, so it is not a fundamental unit. Statement II is a result of $F = ma$, Newton's second law, which is true. If $F = 0$ N, then the acceleration is 0 m/s^2. If the acceleration is 0 m/s^2, then the speed is 0 m/s or a nonzero constant. This is a nonverbal statement of Newton's first law, meaning Newton's first law can be derived from his second law. Newton's second law cannot be derived from the universal law of gravity.

23. B: Electricity requires a generator to make it flow. It needs a conductor as a medium through which it can travel from place to place. An insulator {(A), (C)} is a material that *blocks* the conduction of electricity. Insulation is used to prevent electricity from going where we do not want it to go—for example, into our bodies. Therefore, (D) is incorrect.

24. A: Lions live in a wide-open area where there are few large objects to hide behind. In order to get close enough to their prey to chase and attack it, they must be able to sneak up on it. Their coloration is similar to the color of the tall grasses where they live. This allows the lions to blend into their surroundings and get close to their prey.

25. B: The placenta secretes progesterone and estrogen once a pregnancy is established. The placenta secretes hCG early in pregnancy and in small doses throughout the pregnancy.

26. C: Heat transfer can never occur from a cooler object to a warmer object. While the second law of thermodynamics implies that heat never spontaneously transfers from a cooler object to a warmer object, it is possible for heat to be transferred to a warmer object, given the proper input of work to the system. This is the principle by which a refrigerator operates. Work is done to the system to transfer heat from the objects inside the refrigerator to the air surrounding the refrigerator. All other answer choices are true.

27. C: Catalysts lower the energy barrier between products and reactants and thus increase the reaction rate. Catalysts do not change the thermodynamic position of equilibrium, reaction temperature, or product purity on their own.

28. D: The physical structure of the universe is thought to consist of filaments (walls of superclusters, clusters, and galaxies) that surround large, bubble-like voids. Filaments are the largest structures in the universe, with some forming huge structures like the Great Wall and the Sloan Great Wall.

29. B: The fact that rubrics combine learning objectives, tasks, guidance to students for performing those tasks, and criteria (A) for evaluating student task performance is an advantage they have as assessment tools. Rubrics use a combined set of criteria to try to make an objective assessment of something that is more subjective, such as a performance or presentation. A rubric is very helpful for grounding the grading of a variety of work that students can turn in, but it still is not as objective as something that uses standard, calculated grades. The fact that the performance levels teachers assign are not as precise as number or letter grades or percentages (B) is a disadvantage. The fact that they are brief in nature (C) is an advantage for both students and teachers. The fact that they are both more concise and clearer than many other assessment tools (D) is another advantage.

30. B: Water can stabilize the temperature of living things because of its high specific heat capacity, which means that it takes a while to heat or cool. This ability to minimize changes in temperature protects the body from sudden temperature shifts that could disrupt normal physiological processes. While water does help decrease body temperature through evaporation, this is not a comprehensive description of water's overall role in temperature regulation.

31. A: The troposphere contains three-quarters of the atmosphere's mass and almost all of its water vapor. It is followed by the stratosphere, which is separated from the outermost ionosphere by the mesosphere.

32. B: When more than one gene contributes to a trait, inheritance of that trait is said to be polygenic. This type of inheritance does not follow the rules of Mendelian genetics. Pleiotropy is the opposite, which one gene contributes to two or more unrelated traits. Codominace is a non-Mendelian inheritance where both alleles are expressed in a heterozygote individual, rather than the dominant allele being expressed and the recessive being masked. Gene linkage occurs between two genes that are located near each other on a chromosome and are usually inherited together.

33. C: A parasite is an organism that feeds off the nutritional assets of another living thing called the host, which can lead to the host becoming malnourished or dying. Symbiosis occurs when there is a benefit to both organisms. A predator eats its prey. A producer produces food in the form of plant material that is eaten by a consumer.

34. C: Plants exchange gases with the environment through pores in their leaves called stomata. Animals exchange gases with the environment in many different ways: small animals like flatworms exchange gases through their skin; insects use tracheae; and many species use lungs.

35. A: The First Law of Thermodynamics states that neither matter nor energy can be created or destroyed. They can only be converted from one form to the other. Therefore, matter and energy are always conserved. The Second Law of Thermodynamics is the law of entropy: Energy moves away from its source, which means energy, or heat, cannot flow from a colder to a hotter body. The

Third Law of Thermodynamics states that all energy processes cease as temperature approaches absolute zero. There is a "Zeroth" Law of Thermodynamics (if each of two systems is in equilibrium with a third system, the first two are in equilibrium with each other), but there is no "Fourth Law of Thermodynamics."

36. C: Pollination is the transfer of pollen from the anther, the male part of the flower, to the stigma, the female part of the flower. This transfer can be accomplished either by wind, animals, or water. None of the other choices are involved in pollination: the xylem and petiole are structural and transport tissues; the apical and floral meristems are growth regions; root hairs absorb water and stroma is part of the chloroplast.

37. B: Proteins in the inner membrane of the mitochondrion accept high-energy electrons from NADH and $FADH_2$ and, in turn, transport protons from the matrix to the intermembrane space. The high proton concentration in the intermembrane space creates a gradient, which is harnessed by ATP synthase to produce ATP.

38. C: A general rule of thumb for solubility is "like dissolves like". Polar solutes tend to dissolve in polar solvents, such as water. Nonpolar solutes tend to dissolve in nonpolar solvents. Since CCl_4 has a tetrahedral shape with the polar covalent bonds arranged symmetrically around the carbon atom, CCl_4 is a nonpolar molecule, which should dissolve in a nonpolar solvent. Since $AgNO_3$, NH_3, and KI are polar molecules, they probably won't dissolve in a nonpolar solvent.

39. B: Secondary succession occurs when a habitat has been entirely or partially disturbed or destroyed by abandonment, burning, storms, etc.

40. C: According to the kinetic theory of matter, the kinetic energy of a particle is found by $KE = \frac{1}{2}mv^2$ in which KE is the kinetic energy in Joules, m is the mass of the particle in kilograms, and v is the velocity of the particle in meters per second squared. This formula shows that the average kinetic energy is directly proportional to the square of the average velocity of the particles.

41. C: As the temperature drops to –5 °C, the water vapor condenses to a liquid, and then to a solid. The vapor pressure of a solid is much less than that of the corresponding gas. The argon is still a gas at –5 °C, so almost all the pressure in the cylinder is due to argon.

42. B: The nitrogen is missing its lone pair of electrons, and should have two dots above it. A correct Lewis structure shows how the atoms are connected to each other as well as all of the valence electrons in the compound, so the abbreviated methyl group is also incorrect.

43. D: Electrons trapped by the chlorophyll P680 molecule in photosystem II are energized by light. They are then transferred to electron acceptors in an electron transport chain.

44. A: The lithification process results in the formation of sedimentary rocks. During lithification, existing rock is compacted and liquid is squeezed from its pores. Eventually, the rock is cemented together, resulting in sedimentary rock.

45. B: Newton's First law of motion states *both* that an object at rest tends to stay at rest (A), and an object in motion tends to stay in motion (C), unless or until an opposing force changes this. Newton's *Third law of motion* states that for every action there is an equal and opposite reaction (D).

46. D: Operons are common in prokaryotes. They are units of DNA that control the transcription of DNA and code for their own regulatory proteins as well as structural proteins.

47. B: An independent variable is something that is changed in the experiment. It is being tested against other similar things. In this experiment, the independent variable is the type of window cleaner.

48. C: The question asks how much friction is needed to start the block moving, which means you need to calculate the force of static friction. If the question had asked about the force needed to keep the object moving at a constant speed, you would calculate the force of kinetic friction. Here, the force of static friction is equal to $\mu_{\text{static}} \times N$, where N is the Normal force. The normal force (N) on the plastic block is the weight of the block $(w = mg)$ which is 10 kg × 9.8 m/s^2 = 98 newtons. The force of static friction is 0.6 × 98 N = 59 N. Answer B is the force of kinetic friction, once the block starts moving. (Note: molecular bonding and abrasion cause friction. When the surfaces are in motion, the bonding is less strong, so the coefficient of kinetic friction is less than the coefficient of static friction. Therefore, more force is required to start the box moving than to keep it moving.)

49. A: When two tectonic plates are moving laterally in opposing directions, this is called a transform boundary. When there is friction at transform boundaries and pressure builds up, it can result in shallow earthquakes (usually at a depth of less than 25 meters). California's San Andreas Fault is an example of a transform boundary.

50. C: Giving the students an active task, such as taking notes, will force the students to focus on the content of the tour. Answer A will do little to change or inspire the students to pay more attention. Answer B also has little to do with what students get out of the experience. Answer D is backwards. Having a quiz after the field trip would make more sense.

51. A: Orange red stars have temperatures less than 3,700 K. Yellow orange stars range between 3,700 and 5,200 K. Yellow white stars range between 5,200 and 6,000 K. Blue white stars range between 10,000 and 30,000 K.

52. A: Archimedes, a Greek thinker, contributed to many fields of study during his lifetime (287-212 BC). He studied and wrote about mathematics and various sciences such as physics, engineering, and astronomy. His studies of geometry and mathematics, combined with his observations of the physical world, yielded many inventions and scientific discoveries that have spanned thousands of years. Galilei (1564-1642 AD) is often hailed as the 'father of modern science,' having made significant inroads in the fields of astronomy and physics. Newton (1643-1727 AD), while best known for his Laws of Motion, was a respected figure in many branches of scientific study. Kuo (1031-1085) was a Chinese scientist famous for his work in geology, geomorphology (land formations), zoology, botany, and cartography, simply to name a few.

53. B: A properly adjusted flame should be nearly colorless or blue with an inner and outer cone. If the flame is yellow, increase the air supply. If the flame burns noisily, reduce the gas supply.

54. C: Vectors have a magnitude (e.g., 5 meters/second) and direction (e.g., towards north). Of the choices listed, only velocity is defined as a vector. Speed, distance, and time are all quantities that have a size but not a direction. That's why, for example, a car's speedometer reads 35 miles/hour, but does not indicate your direction of travel.

55. C: Avogadro's number is the number of particles in one mole of a substance. Avogadro's number is 6.022×10^{23}. One mole of any substance contains 6.022×10^{23} particles of that substance.

56. D: Isotopes are variations of an element that have different numbers of neutrons. The various isotopes of an element have the same numbers of protons and electrons. For example, carbon has three naturally occurring isotopes: carbon-12, carbon-13 and carbon-14 (which is radioactive).

Isotopes of an element differ in mass number, which is the number of protons and neutrons added together, but have the same atomic number, or number of protons.

57. D: Respiration produces carbon dioxide and water. The net equation of respiration is the reverse of the equation for photosynthesis. Respiration is a series of reactions that consume glucose and oxygen to release energy and produce carbon dioxide and water. Oxygen and glucose are the substances that are broken down in respiration.

58. A: An inch is about 2.54 cm $= 25.4$ mm $= 2.54 \times 10^{-5}$ km $= 2.54 \times 10^{-2}$ m.

59. C: In respiration, food is used to produce energy as glucose and oxygen that react to produce carbon dioxide, water and ATP

60. A: By comparing the products to the reactants, there must be at least two Al atoms in the starting material, and at least three sulfate groups. Therefore, a coefficient of 2 must be placed in front of $Al(OH)_3$ and a coefficient of 3 must be placed in front of H_2SO_4. To make the number of hydrogen and oxygen atoms equal on both sides of the equation, a coefficient of 6 must be placed in front of H_2O.

61. A: Chemical composition is not one of the physical properties used to classify minerals. The five major physical properties used to classify minerals are luster, hardness, cleavage, streak, and form. There is a separate classification system based on the chemical composition of minerals.

62. A: Cations are positively charged ions. Anions are negatively charged ions; therefore, the ion Ca^{2+} is a cation. Cations are positively charged because they have lost one or more electrons. This cation has lost two electrons and has fewer electrons than protons.

63. C: In the stratosphere, temperature increases as altitude increases. The stratosphere contains the ozone layer, which absorbs ultraviolet radiation and then reemits this energy as heat.

64. B: One of the key concepts of biodiversity is the interconnectedness of living things. If students are visiting a natural environment, they will observe plants, animals, air and water phenomenon, as well as any non-natural environmental factors. In keeping a field journal, students will deepen their understanding of all these factors. Ideally, they will also start to note the relationships between living things and understand that none of them would survive without the others. Noting the relationships and effects organisms have upon one another will be an important part of keeping their journals.

65. B: A guyot is defined as a seamount with a flattened top. The term "seamount" refers to any undersea volcano that is more than 1,000 meters tall. Undersea troughs are called trenches, and undersea mountain chains are called mid-ocean ridges.

66. A: Since there are 7 moles of neon out of a total of 14 moles of gas in the cylinder, the partial pressure of neon will always be 50% of the total pressure, regardless of the temperature.

67. C: To determine if this bat is from a particular species, the remains must be compared with the remains of the other members of the species.

68. D: Since the atomic number of this isotope is 92, the atom contains 92 protons. Since the mass number is 238, the atom contains 238 protons and neutrons. Since the difference between 238 and 92 is 146, the atom contains 146 neutrons.

69. D: A chemical reaction will always have an endothermic (absorb energy) or exothermic (release energy) reaction, and a chemical formula must always be balanced. Therefore, the masses of the reactants and products will always be equal, resulting in the modification of the atoms arrangement and a change in energy.

70. B: A decrease in a natural predator, such as a wolves, coyotes, bobcat, or wild dogs, would allow the population to become out of control. In a population of deer that has increased, there would be a natural decrease in a food source for the nutritional needs for the animals. Although deer have been known to share a human's developed habitat, it is often forced by reduced territory and food sources. An increase in hunting licenses would be used by local officials to try to control the population, helping to decrease the number of adults of breeding age.

71. C: An irrigation scheme that draws water from a river and redistributes the water in the local area leads to an increase in evaporation, not a decrease. This is largely due to the increase of the surface area of contact of the water and the atmosphere.

72. B: Mass is the amount of matter in an object. Weight is the measure of the pull of gravity on an object.

73. C: As the amplitude of the pendulum increases due to resonance, it will swing higher. However, the period of a pendulum is not connected to how high it swings. Only the length of the pendulum affects its period. The length of a pendulum will not be affected by how high it's swinging or whether it's in resonance.

74. A: Isotopes are two atoms of the same element that have different mass. They have the same number of protons but a different number of neutrons. Choice C accurately describes ions. The other choices are incorrect.

75. D: DNA is composed of nucleotides joined together in long chains. Nucleotides are composed of a pentose sugar, a phosphate group, and a nitrogenous base. The bases form the "rungs" of the ladder at the core of the DNA helix, and the pentose-phosphates are on its outside, or backbone.

76. A: Since 1 g is equal to 1,000 mg, 2,310 mg is equivalent to 2.310 g. Since 1 kg is equal to 1,000 g, 2.310 kg is equivalent to 2,310 g, and 2.310 kg is equivalent to 2,310,000 mg.

77. C: The ice skaters are applying Newton's Third Law to create an equal and opposite reaction force, causing both partners to move. Although each skater is pushing the other, there is another force that must be considered in that they moved as well.

78. B: The Biological Species Concept (BSC) states that the status of "species" is based on the natural reproductive isolation of populations. Populations that could potentially interbreed and produce fertile offspring but do not do so in nature are considered different species under the BSC. This species concept does not consider the ability to interbreed under artificial conditions: if two groups do not breed with one another for any reason (in nature), they are reproductively isolated and therefore different species according to the BSC. The isolation may be due to geography, behavior, appearance, or other factors. For example, the Eastern and Western meadowlark look very similar and have overlapping territories, but they have different songs. Individual meadowlarks identify others by their songs and only breed with those with the same song. Because the two populations are reproductively isolated from one another, they are considered different species under the BSC. If individuals with different songs did interbreed and produce fertile offspring, they would be considered the same species.

79. C: In physics, systematic errors occur when comparing a theoretical value with an experimental value. The experimental value differed from the actual by 2.1 pounds, which is the systematic error. Since there is always random error, Answer A is incorrect. But random error is just that — random— so it cannot be 2.1 pound, which is systematic because it's a consistent error due to the method used to take this measurement.

80. B: Genetics encompasses the concept of traits and how certain traits are passed from parents to offspring. The traits listed in the left-hand column are commonly studied in the field of genetics, as they are passed down based upon combinations of recessive and dominant genes. Choices A and C are not directly related to the chart. Choice D refers to the process by which organisms adapt to the environment. However, the traits listed in this chart are not vital to the survival of a species, making choice B a better fit.

81. D: Expansion in the redshifts of galaxies, measurements of cosmic microwave background radiation, and measurements of the distribution of quasars and galaxies are all considered observational evidence in support of the Big Bang Theory. The abundance of certain "primordial elements" is also consistent with the theory.

82. C: Crossing the corresponding alleles from each parent will yield a result of BB in the upper right box of this Punnett square.

83. A: Heat capacity refers to the amount of heat or thermal energy required to raise the temperature of a specific substance by a given unit. A substance with a higher heat capacity requires more heat to raise its temperature than a substance with a lower heat capacity. The comparison here is that the specific heat capacity of ice is half as much as that of liquid water, so it takes half the amount of energy to increase the same amount of ice one temperature unit than it would if it were liquid water.

84. B: A physical change refers to one in which the substance being acted upon maintains its chemical composition. Thus, any change in which a substance melts, freezes, or evaporates is a physical change, as is one in which the substance simply changes its shape. A chemical change is one in which the substance changes in chemical substance. The only choice in which a new chemical entity is formed is that in which rust forms on a nail.

85. A: The sky looks blue because of Rayleigh scattering, in which air molecules scatter short-wavelength light, especially blue, much more than longer wavelengths. This scattered blue light reaches our eyes from all directions, making the sky look blue. Therefore (B) is incorrect. Glass appears transparent to us; however, it is really only transparent to the light frequencies (wavelengths) that we can see, but to ultraviolet light frequencies, which we cannot see, glass is actually opaque. Wood, metal, and other materials look opaque to us *not* because they reflect light (D) but rather because they absorb light.

86. C: Covalent compounds are usually formed by the combination of two or more non-metallic elements with one another. In these compounds, atoms share electrons. Ionic compounds are most often formed between a metal and a nonmetal. Organic compounds are covalent compounds that contain carbon and hydrogen atoms. Some of the compounds formed by non-metallic elements are polar, but not all of them.

87. D: Nonvascular plants do not produce seeds like angiosperms and gymnosperms do. They generally reproduce sexually, but produce spores instead of seeds.

88. B: Flowers are the reproductive organs of a plant. Flowering plants reproduce by sexual reproduction where the gametes join to form seeds. Pollen is sperm. Pollinators help transfer the sperm to the ovule, by way of the stigma. The style is the part of the female reproduction system that transports the sperm between the stigma and the ovary, which are all parts of the pistil. The stigma is the sticky tip of the style on which the pollen lands. Sepals are usually small leaves between or underneath the petals and are not as obvious or as large and colorful as the petals.

89. B: Venus experiences a greenhouse effect similar to that observed on Earth as its dense atmosphere traps the solar radiation and creates a greenhouse effect. The greenhouse gases, including ozone, carbon dioxide, water vapor, and methane, trap infrared radiation that is reflected back toward the atmosphere. While both Venus and Earth experience the greenhouse effect, Venus's greenhouse effect is much more severe. Earth, on the other hand, has many more natural convective processes that help move carbon and other gases around, tempering the effect some. Human activity produces byproducts that contribute to the greenhouse effect. Some practices that increase the amount of greenhouse gases are burning natural gas and oil; farming, which leads to more methane and nitrous oxide; deforestation, which decreases the amount of offset oxygen; and population growth in general, which increases the volume of greenhouse gases. Increased gases mean more infrared radiation is trapped. While the greenhouse effect is not itself debated, the long-term effects tend to be hotly debated among scientists and in political agendas.

90. B: A total solar eclipse can be observed only by viewers located within the umbra. The umbra is the darkest part of the shadow, and the light source is not visible from it. The penumbra is the lighter portion of the shadow from which the light source is partially visible. In a solar eclipse, the Moon passes between the Earth and the Sun, and viewers in the umbra experience a total solar eclipse.

91. D: The three layers of the heart are the epicardium (outermost), myocardium (middle), and endocardium (innermost). "Vasocardium" is not a layer of the heart or even a legitimate term. The adjectives "vasocardial" or "vasocardiac" are used to refer to anything related to both blood vessels (vaso-) and heart (cardiac), as with the "vasocardial system." A related term with the order of parts reversed is "cardiovascular system."

92. A: Learner-centered assessment provides alternatives that allow different students to be assessed differently. Although student participation in assessment creation (D) is also an important part of learner-centered assessment, a multiple choice test does not reflect the goals of learner-centered assessment because it does not provide an authentic assessment experience.

93. B: Making a determination based on the results of a controlled experiment is a description of concluding. Inferring can be described as explaining or interpreting observations. Reading an instrument during an experiment is one type of quantitative observation. Comparing includes noting similarities and differences.

94. C: Human activities have not influenced the increased population of all species but have all played a role in the other environmental issues. As wetlands are degraded or lost, many ecosystems and species will also be lost, interrupting their respective food webs. Food webs within the actual oceans will also be reduced due to pollution and climate changes that impact water temperatures and levels. The diminishment of coral reefs means the ocean's water filtration system will be reduced or totally destroyed, affecting the ecosystems themselves as well as the organisms that use the area for breeding and feeding.

95. C: The main human-caused reason for "dead zones" in portions of oceans and lakes that normally host abundant aquatic life is the use of chemical fertilizers. These fertilizers, which are high in nitrogen and phosphorous, enter lakes and rivers in water runoff and become concentrated in certain areas. This concentration, called eutrophication, eventually depletes the water's oxygen levels and renders it incapable of supporting life.

96. C: In order to pinpoint the exact location of the epicenter, seismograms are needed from three widely separate locations. A circle is drawn around each location with a radius equal to the distance of the earthquake. Since two circles can cross in two locations, a third circle is needed to pinpoint which intersection is the location of the epicenter. The intersection of the three circles is the location of the epicenter.

97. D: Endocytosis is a process by which cells absorb larger molecules or even tiny organisms, such as bacteria, that would not be able to pass through the plasma membrane. Endocytic vesicles containing molecules from the extracellular environment often undergo further processing once they enter the cell.

98. C: Metalloids have some properties of metals and some properties of nonmetals. A good semiconductor has the conductive properties of metals and a stability at high temperatures that is characteristic of nonmetals.

99. D: Conjugation is direct transfer of plasmid DNA between bacteria through a pilus. The F plasmid contains genes that enable bacteria to produce pili and is often the DNA that is transferred between bacteria.

100. C: All three laws of motion are operating, but the third law (forces come in equal and opposite pairs) best explains the motion. The first law (inertia) is shown from the fact that the balloon doesn't move until a force acts upon it. The second law (F = ma) is shown because you can see the force and the acceleration. The force comes from the contraction of the rubber balloon. The stretched rubber exerts a force on the air inside the balloon. This causes the air to accelerate in accordance with the second law. You can't see this acceleration because the air is invisible and because it is all the air in the room that the balloon is exerting a force on. However, the air in the room exerts an equal and opposite force on the balloon (this is Newton's third law), which causes the balloon to accelerate in the direction it did.

101. D: Diamagnetic materials align perpendicularly to magnetic field lines, and do not retain magnetic properties when the external magnetic field is removed. These include copper, silver, gold, and most other elements in the periodic table. Paramagnetic (C) materials align parallel to magnetic field lines, and also do not retain magnetic properties upon removal of the external field. These include lithium, magnesium, molybdenum, and tantalum. Ferromagnetic (B) materials retain their magnetic properties even when the external magnetic field is removed. These include iron, nickel, and cobalt. Magnetic induction (A) is the name for the process whereby magnets turn magnetic substances near them into magnets as well.

102. A: Carbohydrates are the primary source of energy for the body. Proteins and lipids also provide energy, but are not as readily digestible to use actively. The Dietary Guidelines for Americans recommend that 45-65% of food intake consist of carbohydrates. Vitamins and minerals aid in metabolism and allow for cellular repair. Fats and proteins are available for energy if the body needs them, but the primary function of fats is to support cell growth and regulation of bodily functions, while the primary function of proteins is to help repair and build muscle tissue and to regulate chemical balances in the body.

103. C: Chloroplasts contain the light-absorbing compound chlorophyll, which is essential in photosynthesis. This gives leaves their green color. Chloroplasts also contain yellow and red carotenoid pigments, which give leaves red and yellow colors in the fall as chloroplasts lose their chlorophyll.

104. C: Chemicals should not be stored routinely on bench tops. Each chemical should be stored in a location for that specific type of chemical. When in use, chemicals may be temporarily kept on bench tops, but only in the quantities that are required for that particular situation. Chemicals should be returned to an appropriate location after use.

105. D: Lead (Pb) goes from a 0 oxidation state to a 2+ oxidation state, and is therefore oxidized. Oxidation is the loss of electrons. Hydrogen goes from a 1+ oxidation state to a 0 oxidation state, and is therefore reduced. Reduction is the gaining of electrons.

106. D: Stomata are openings on leaves that allow for gas exchange, which is essential for photosynthesis. Stomata are surrounded by guard cells, which open and close based on their turgidity.

107. D: *Transpiration* is the primary process responsible for the bulk passage of water through a plant. It describes the evaporation of water from the leaves, which causes negative pressure that pulls water upward from the roots. Cohesion, adhesion, and osmosis all support this process. *Cohesion* is the attractive force between two molecules of the same substance. *Adhesion* is the attractive force between molecules of different substances. *Osmosis* is a process in which water diffuses through a selectively permeable membrane.

108. C: Producers always form the base of an energy pyramid as the first trophic level. Each successive level receives about 10% of the energy from the previous level. In this energy pyramid, the second trophic level receives 10% of 6,000 or 600 kilocalories per square meter per year. The third trophic level receives 10% of 600, or 60 kilocalories per square meter per year.

109. C: Insertions and deletions cause frameshift mutations. These mutations cause all subsequent nucleotides to be displaced by one position, and thereby cause all the amino acids to be different than they would have been if the mutation had not occurred.

110. C: Displacement is a vector that indicates the change in the location of an object. Answer A would be correct if the question asked for the total distance the person walked or if the person didn't change direction. If the person turned around 180°, the displacement could be as small as 5 meters. If the person changed directions only a fraction of a degree, the displacement's magnitude would be *less* than 13 meters, not as *large* as 13 meters.

111. D: Enzymes are substrate-specific. Most enzymes catalyze only one biochemical reaction. Their active sites are specific for a certain type of substrate and do not bind to other substrates and catalyze other reactions.

112. D: Combustion of coal releases significant amounts of Hg into the atmosphere. When the Hg settles into the water, it becomes methylated and concentrates in fish, making them toxic to eat.

113. B: While land reclamation destroys nearby habitats, it doesn't increase biodiversity. The destruction of habitats leads to a decrease in biodiversity.

114. D: Darwin introduced his idea of natural selection in *On the Origin of Species*, in which he stated that nature selects the best-adapted varieties to survive and reproduce. Lamarck wrote

Philosophie Zoologique, in which he proposed a theory of inheritance of acquired characteristics. This theory states that if an organism changes during its life to adapt to its environment, those changes are passed on to its offspring. Lyell wrote *Principles of Geology*, in which he introduced his idea of uniformitarianism, which states that the geological processes that alter the earth are uniform through time. Malthus wrote *An Essay on the Principle of Population*, in which he stated that human populations will rapidly increase unless kept in check by limits in food supply.

115. B: Electrons, protons, and neutrons are subatomic particles. Electrons have the smallest mass. Protons and neutrons, which are nearly equal in mass, are several orders of magnitude more massive than electrons. Quarks are believed to be the components of protons and neutrons; while a quark has less mass than a complete proton or neutron, it still has more mass than an electron.

116. B: The moment of inertia of a point mass, m, about any axis is given by mR^2, where R is the distance from the axis. The moment of inertia of a solid object is calculated by imagining that the object is made up of point masses and adding the moments of inertia of the point masses. The average radius of the particles in a hollow cylinder will be R (all the mass is at radius R). For a solid cylinder, however, the average radius is less than R, meaning the overall moment of inertia will be smaller. The moment of inertia of a cylinder of thickness $R_2 - R_1$, where R_1 and R_2 are the inner and outer radii, respectively, is calculated by $\frac{1}{2}m({R_1}^2 + {R_2}^2)$. For a solid cylinder, $R_1 = 0$ meters. For a hollow cylinder, $R_1 = R_2$.

117. C: Minerals that form on the sea floor from discarded shells are most likely part of the carbonate class. Minerals that form in karst regions and evaporitic settings may also be carbonates. Examples of minerals in the carbonate class include aragonite, dolomite, calcite, and siderite.

118. C: Protons and neutrons are both considered nucleons. The number of nucleons in a nucleus is called the mass number. Isotopes of the same element have different mass numbers. But since they are the same element, they must have the same atomic number, which is equal to the number of protons. Thus, only the number of neutrons changes, since electron's mass is so low that it doesn't have much effect on the mass number of an element. Unless they are also ionized, they would have the same number of protons and electrons.

119. A: The field of view is the diameter of the circle of light that is seen when one looks into the microscope. As the power of the objective increases, the field of view gets smaller. Therefore, the objective with the greatest field of view is the one with the lowest power.

120. A: Newton's first law (inertia) says an object in motion stays in motion, and an object at rest stays at rest, unless external forces act on them. Choice A is an excellent demonstration because it shows the ball at rest and in motion. At rest, the ball stays at rest until a force acts on it. When the ball is moving, there is no force acting on the ball in the direction of motion. Thus, the natural state of the ball is to be at rest or moving with a constant speed. Choice C is not a good demonstration because the force of friction is what makes it hard to move the heavy object. Choice B is a good demonstration of equilibrium and friction. Running a current through parallel wires (D) has nothing to do with Newton's first law.

121. C: Sources of renewable energy include geothermal power, solar energy, and wind power. Sources of nonrenewable energy include nuclear power and fossil fuels like coal, natural gas, and crude oil.

122. C: Cell layers and cell shape are the criteria for classifying epithelial tissue.

123. C: Reduction takes place at the cathode and oxidation takes place at the anode. Mg^{2+} of the salt will be reduced to Mg at the cathode, and Cl^- will be oxidized to Cl_2 at the anode.

124. B: Fission occurs when the nucleus breaks up into two smaller nuclei. When certain nuclear isotopes absorb a neutron, they become unstable and split, starting the process of fission. The average binding energy per nucleon increases with a fission reaction, and the two new nuclei are more stable than the initial nucleus. The increase in binding energy comes from the changes in mass of the protons and neutrons (note: both protons and neutrons are nucleons). The release of energy is part of the fission reaction, but this does not explain why the fission reaction occurs.

125. B: If a gas and a liquid are placed in a sealed container, cooling the liquid will help dissolve the gas into the liquid. Gases have higher solubility in liquids at lower temperatures. At higher temperatures, the gas molecules will have more kinetic energy and will have enough energy to overcome intermolecular interactions with the liquid solvent and leave the solution. This also explains why heating the liquid is incorrect. Shaking the container is also incorrect as this would give the gas energy to escape. Decreasing the pressure on the lid may or may not significantly affect the pressure inside the vessel depending on the nature of the vessel, but decreasing the pressure inside the vessel would decrease the solubility of the gas in the liquid.

126. B: The Cambrian explosion occurred during the Cambrian Period in the Paleozoic Era, approximately 541,000,000 years ago. The Jurassic Period, known for the first giant dinosaurs, occurred during the Mesozoic Era and began approximately 201,000,000 years ago.

127. C: Hybridization between two different species would result in more genetic variation than sexual reproduction within a species.

128. D: Within a habitat, there is a maximum number of individuals that can continue to thrive, known as the habitat's carrying capacity. When the population size approaches this number, population growth will stop.

129. A: The chromosomes separate during anaphase and move to the opposite ends of the cells.

130. D: Chalk is a form of calcium carbonate, which has the molecular formula $CaCO_3$.

131. B: Solubility is the amount of solute present in saturated solution. For a gas solute in a liquid solvent, increasing the temperature increases the kinetic energy of the gas molecules, which decreases the solubility of the gas in the liquid. Increasing the pressure of the gas increases the number of particles escaping from the surface and increases the solubility. For a solid solute in a liquid solvent, increasing the temperature increases the kinetic energy, which increases the number of collisions and increases the solubility. Increasing the pressure of a solid solute in a liquid has little or no effect on solubility.

132. D: Benefits to using fossil fuels include that they are cheap and reliable and relatively safe to extract. The technology to control pollution is already developed. The most serious drawback to using fossil fuels is that their pollution contributes greatly to global warming.

133. A: Bernoulli's principle states that the lateral pressure exerted by a moving fluid decreases as the fluid's speed increases. This principle is named after Daniel Bernoulli.

134. B: Vibration is caused by anything physical moving rapidly back and forth. When an object vibrates, the vibrations disturb the medium surrounding it, which may be solid matter, liquids, or gases like the air. Sound does not cause vibrations in the air (A) but vice versa: vibrations are a type of energy. The sound caused by vibration is acoustic energy, and vibratory movements disturb their medium, like the air. Sound causes vibrations not only in the air, but also in the ear (C) when they reach it. Whereas sound waves traveling through the air and through the outer and middle ear are acoustic energy, once they reach the inner ear, it converts that acoustic energy into electrical energy that is sent via nerves to the brain (D).

135. C: When salt water penetrates fractures in rocks and leaves behind salt crystals that cause the rock to fracture, it is considered physical rather than chemical weathering. Chemical weathering involves changes in the molecules that make up the rocks, while physical weathering occurs when external factors act on the rock without changing its chemical composition in any way.

136. B: When the angle of incidence is zero, the angle of refraction is also zero. As the angle of incidence increases, the angle of refraction increases. When the angle of incidence reaches the critical angle, the angle of refraction is 90 degrees. When the angle of incidence is greater than the critical angle, the light undergoes total internal reflection. No light is refracted.

137. C: 100 g of HBr equals 1.23 moles, and 100 g of Mg equals 4.11 moles. From the coefficients of the balanced equation, the ratio of HBr to Mg is 2 : 1. This means that to react 1.23 moles of HBr, 2.46 moles of Mg would be required. Since 4.11 moles of Mg are present, Mg is in excess.

138. D: The amount of potential energy an object has depends on mass, height above ground and gravitational attraction, but not temperature. The formula for potential energy is $PE = mgh$, or potential energy equals mass times gravity times height. Answers (A), (B), and (C) are all valid answers as they are all contained in the formula for potential energy. Potential energy is the amount of energy stored in a system particularly because of its position.

139. D: Gravitational collapse and high-energy collisions are both proposed explanations for the formation of black holes. Gravitational collapse occurs when the outward pressure exerted by an object is too weak to resist that object's own gravity. Collisions that produce conditions of sufficient density could also, in theory, create black holes. The accretion of matter is considered observational evidence for the existence of black holes.

140. B: An iron bar moving inside a coil of wire that contains a current would create an electromagnet. Rapidly spinning and rotating electrons inside an iron bar (A) creates a magnetic field. The movement of electrons through a complete circuit (C) is an electric current. Convection currents within the liquid core of Earth's interior (D) create the Earth's magnetic field.

Practice Test #2

1. All of the following are examples of metamorphic rocks EXCEPT:

a. Granite
b. Quartzite
c. Slate
d. Marble

2. How does meiosis differ from mitosis?

a. Meiosis is used to repair the body. Mitosis is used to break down the body.
b. Meiosis is used for asexual reproduction of single-celled organisms. Mitosis is used for sexual reproduction of multicellular organisms.
c. Meiosis only occurs in humans. Mitosis only occurs in plants.
d. Meiosis produces cells that are genetically different. Mitosis produces cells that are genetically identical.

3. What will happen to light waves as they hit a convex lens?

a. They will be refracted and converge.
b. They will be refracted and diverge.
c. They will be reflected and converge.
d. They will be reflected and diverge.

4. Which of the following is NOT a true statement about how batteries work?

a. A battery works by completing a circuit within an electrical device.
b. Batteries store energy in the form of chemical energy.
c. The cathode is the reducing agent.
d. Electrons are lost at the anode.

5. What does it mean when someone says that electric charge is conserved?

a. Like charges repel, and unlike charges attract.
b. The net charge of an isolated system remains constant.
c. Charges come from electrons and protons.
d. Charge can never be created or destroyed.

6. Which of the following is not an advantage angiosperms show over other types of plants?

a. Larger leaves
b. Double fertilization
c. Dormant seeds
d. Lower seed dispersal

7. Which of the following statements is NOT true?

a. The Earth rotates on its axis once every 24 hours
b. A solar eclipse can only occur during a new moon
c. The Moon rotates on its axis as it revolves around the Earth
d. A lunar eclipse occurs when the Moon passes between the Earth and the Sun

Refer to the following for questions 8–9:

Let B represent the dominant allele for a full head of hair, and let b represent the recessive allele for male-pattern baldness. The following Punnett square represents the offspring of two people with recessive genes for baldness.

	B	b
B	Possibility 1	Possibility 2
b	Possibility 3	Possibility 4

8. According to the Punnett square, which possibility would produce an offspring with a full head of hair?

a. Possibility 1
b. Possibility 2
c. Possibility 3
d. All of the above

9. According to the Punnett square, which possibility would produce an offspring with male-pattern baldness?

a. Possibility 1
b. Possibility 2
c. Possibility 3
d. Possibility 4

10. Which section of the digestive system is responsible for water reabsorption?

a. The large intestine
b. The duodenum
c. The small intestine
d. The gallbladder

11. The volume of water in a bucket is 2.5 liters. When an object with an irregular shape and a mass of 40 grams is fully submerged in the water, the total volume becomes 4.5 liters. What is the density of the object?

a. 0.1 g/L
b. 2 g/L
c. 20 g/L
d. 80 g/L

12. Suppose a moving railroad car collides with an identical stationary car and the two cars latch together. Ignoring friction, and assuming no deformation on impact, which of the following statements is true?

a. The speed of the first car decreases by half.
b. The collision is elastic.
c. The speed of the first car is doubled.
d. There is no determining the final speed because the collision was inelastic.

13. Darwin's idea that evolution occurs by the gradual accumulation of small changes can be described as:

a. Punctuated equilibrium
b. Phyletic gradualism
c. Convergent evolution
d. Adaptive radiation

14. Which of the following factors directly contributes to soil erosion?

a. Air pollution from cars and factories
b. Use of pesticides
c. Deforestation and overgrazing
d. Water pollution caused by excess sedimentation

15. When heat is removed from water during condensation, which of the following are formed.

a. Atoms
b. Covalent bonds
c. Intermolecular bonds
d. Ionic bonds

Refer to the following for question 16:

> *A student is conducting an experiment using a ball that is attached to the end of a string, forming a pendulum. The student pulls the ball back so that it is at an angle to its resting position. As the student releases the ball, it swings forward and backward. The student measures the time it takes the ball to make one complete period. A period is defined as the time it takes the ball to swing forward and back again to its starting position. This is repeated using different string lengths.*

16. The student formed the following hypothesis:

> *Lengthening the string of the pendulum will increase the time it takes the ball to make one complete period.*

What correction would you have the student make to the hypothesis to make it follow the classical hypothesis model?

a. Turn it into an "if/then" statement.
b. Change "will increase" to "increases."
c. Switch the order of the sentence so that the phrase about the period comes first, and the phrase about the string's length is last.
d. No corrections are needed.

17. A weather balloon is filled with 1,000 mol of He gas at 25 °C and 101 kPa of pressure. What is the volume of the weather balloon?

a. 24,518 m^3
b. 24.5 m^3
c. 2 m^3
d. 245 m^3

18. Which of the following is a characteristic of a reputable scientific journal?

a. Peer review of the quality of research
b. Famous scientists on the editorial board
c. Use of color graphics to represent data
d. Statistical analysis of all research data

19. The pulley in the device below has no mass and is frictionless. The larger mass is 30 kg and the smaller mass is 20 kg. What is the acceleration of the masses?

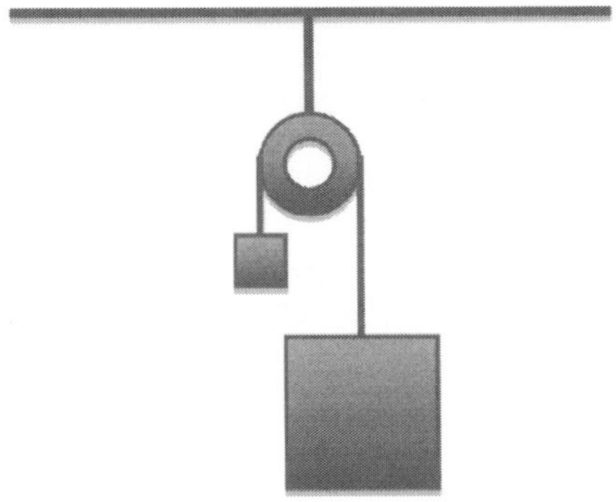

a. $0.5\ m/s^2$
b. $2.0\ m/s^2$
c. $9.8\ m/s^2$
d. $98\ m/s^2$

20. Transverse traveling waves propagate through a taut string of length 20 meters at a speed of 4 m/s. Standing waves are set up in this string which is fixed at both ends. What is the smallest frequency possible for the standing waves?

a. 0.1 Hz
b. 0.05 Hz
c. 0.2 Hz
d. 0.4 Hz

21. Which of Howard Gardner's multiple intelligences would most enable a student to identify rock types for a geology or earth science class?

a. Kinesthetic intelligence
b. Naturalist intelligence
c. Logical-mathematical intelligence
d. Spatial intelligence

22. Approximately 96.5% of seawater is composed of:

a. Hydrogen and sodium
b. Hydrogen and oxygen
c. Oxygen and sodium
d. Chlorine and sodium

23. What is the role of ribosomes?

a. Protein production
b. Waste removal
c. Transport
d. Storage

24. The discovery of X-rays has impacted society on many levels. Which of the following impacts occurred first?

a. Medical imaging
b. Fighting cancer
c. Security scanners
d. Discovering distant galaxies

25. How is meiosis similar to mitosis?

a. Both produce daughter cells that are genetically identical.
b. Both produce daughter cells that are genetically different.
c. Both occur in humans, other animals, and plants.
d. Both occur asexually.

26. What is the name of the compound $CuCl_2$?

a. Copper (I) chloride
b. Copper (II) chloride
c. Copper (I) chlorine
d. Copper (II) chlorine

Refer to the following for questions 27–28:

Diagram of a complete, perfect flower

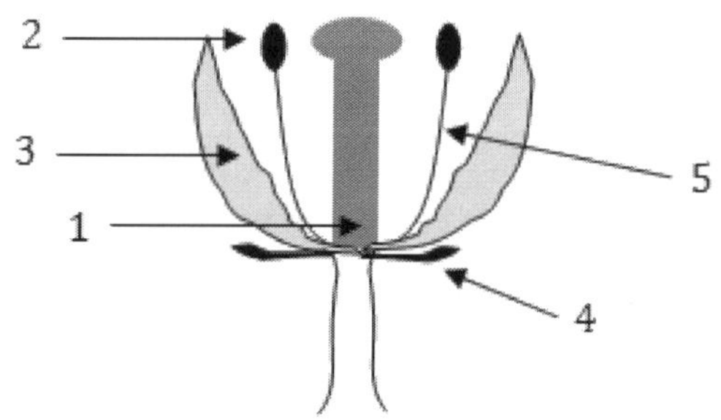

27. The structure in which microspores are produced is:

a. 1
b. 2
c. 3
d. 4

28. Which of the following is NOT considered a reproductive organ of the flower?

a. 1
b. 2
c. 3
d. 4

29. Which of the following situations would result in the generation of new crust?

a. Two crustal plates converge.
b. Two crustal plates move apart.
c. Two crustal plates slide past one another.
d. A crustal plate is pushed down into the mantle.

30. A gas is held in a closed container and held at constant temperature. What is the effect of increasing the volume of the container by 3 times?

a. The pressure is tripled.
b. The pressure increases by one-third.
c. The pressure decreases to one-third.
d. The pressure remains constant.

31. A box with a weight of 10 newtons is resting on a table, which is resting on the ground. In the context of Newton's third law, if we consider the force of the box on the table to be the action force, which of the following statements is true?

a. The force of the table on the box is the reaction force.
b. The force of the table on the ground is the reaction force.
c. The force of the ground on the table is the reaction force.
d. There is no reaction force because the system is in equilibrium.

32. Every year thousands of square miles of trees are cut down to make paper products. Which of the following is not a result of cutting down trees?

a. Animals experience a loss of habitat
b. There is a decrease in the amount of oxygen available
c. There is a decrease in the amount of food available to herbivores and omnivores
d. There is a decrease in the amount of CO_2 in the atmosphere

33. A boy is outside in the winter and notices that he begins shivering when he gets cold. A girl is outside during the summer and begins sweating when she gets hot. Why do the children's bodies react this way?

a. The children's bodies are attempting to regulate their temperature.
b. The children's bodies are trying to fight off disease.
c. The children's bodies are reacting to the amount of sunlight or shade.
d. The children are having an allergic reaction to something in the air.

34. Which of the following statements correctly describes the relationship between temperature and density in water?

a. As the temperature of liquid water decreases, density decreases monotonically.
b. As the temperature of frozen water (ice) increases, density decreases monotonically.
c. Water in the solid state generally has a higher density than water in the liquid state.
d. Water in the liquid state generally has a higher density than water in the solid state.

35. Which graph segment below represents the greatest acceleration?

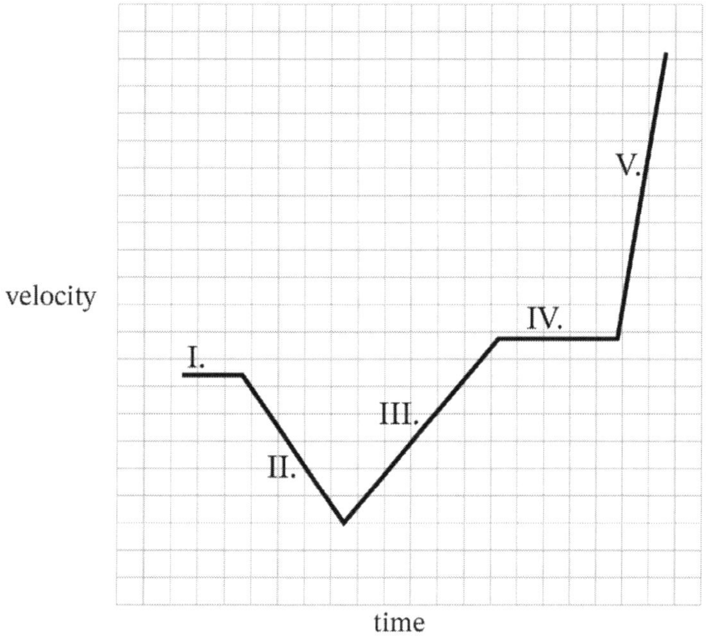

a. II
b. III
c. V
d. III and V

36. Which of the following is true of the enzyme telomerase?

a. It is active on the leading strand during DNA synthesis
b. It requires a chromosomal DNA template
c. It acts in the $3' \rightarrow 5'$ direction
d. It adds a repetitive DNA sequence to the end of chromosomes

37. What happens to the temperature of a substance as it is changing phase from a liquid to a solid?

a. Its temperature increases due to the absorption of latent heat.
b. Its temperature decreases due to the heat of vaporization.
c. Its temperature decreases due to the latent heat of fusion.
d. Its temperature remains the same due to the latent heat of fusion.

Refer to the following for question 38:

Many fishermen will watch the tide report for the local area and get up very early or stay out late in order to have the best fishing opportunity. One night while out late fishing, a fisherman noticed that the land temperature cooled rapidly, while the ocean water stayed relatively warm.

38. Which factor affects the fisherman's fishing opportunities?

a. The gravitational relationship between the earth and moon
b. The gravitational relationship between the earth and sun
c. The earth's gravity
d. The moon's phases

39. How does the loss of biodiversity directly impact the environment and society?

a. Increase of access to raw materials
b. Increase of access to clean water
c. Decrease of food supply
d. Decrease of vulnerability to natural disasters

40. In which taxonomic group are organisms MOST alike?

a. Phylum
b. Family
c. Class
d. Order

41. What is the name of the process by which a bacterial cell splits into two new cells?

a. Mitosis
b. Meiosis
c. Replication
d. Binary fission

42. A science teacher wants to allow the students to investigate which parts of the school have the most bacteria. He splits the students into groups to have them brainstorm where they should test for bacteria and how they should report their findings. Which of the following is the most important reason for having students brainstorm how to do this investigation?

a. It assists the students in determining what they still need to learn to conduct this experiment
b. It allows the students to form positive relationships with their peers in the classroom
c. It helps the teacher determine which students understand the purpose of the experiment and which students need more assistance
d. It helps the students take ownership and become engaged in their learning

43. The center of an atom is called the ____. It is composed of ____.

a. nucleus; protons and neutrons
b. nucleus; protons and electrons
c. electron cloud; electrons and protons
d. electron cloud; electrons and neutrons

44. To make a good buffering system in the pH range of 5-9, which acid/base combinations would likely work the best?

a. $HCl/NaOH$
b. $HNO_3/NaNO_3$
c. $H_2SO_4/NaHSO_4$
d. NaH_2PO_4/Na_2HPO_4

45. Which of the following is a true statement about the Earth's oceans?

a. Oceans comprise about 50% of the Earth's surface.
b. The deepest point in the ocean is about 6,000 meters below sea level.
c. The ocean is divided geographically into four areas: the Atlantic, Pacific, Mediterranean, and Indian.
d. The ocean's salinity is usually between 34 and 35 parts per thousand, or 200 parts per million.

46. Which of the following is a trait that results from disruptive selection?

a. Insecticide resistance
b. Only male peacocks having colorful plumage
c. Some birds having significantly large bills than others within the same species
d. Human height

47. Mr. Harris' science classroom has been recently equipped with ten lab stations, which include a full supply of scientific tools, sinks, hot plates, and more. The students and teachers alike are looking forward to the hands-on activities that Mr. Harris will now be able to provide his young learners. What would be the best possible introductory unit in this scenario?

a. A hands-on demonstration of how the scientific method works in a scientific experiment and written follow-up work on each step in the process.
b. Lessons on various tools and parts of the lab, concentrating on how to use each item safely.
c. Several labs in which the students can witness visible chemical processes, increasing the students' excitement about the lab.
d. A discussion about the process leading up to the installation of the lab, including social science concepts regarding fundraising, interest, etc.

48. A substance has a half-life of 2.4×10^4 years. How long does it take for 87.5% of the substance to decay?

a. 2.1×10^4 years
b. 4.5×10^4 years
c. 7.2×10^4 years
d. 9.6×10^4 years

49. What function do ribosomes serve within the cell?

a. Ribosomes are responsible for cell movement.
b. Ribosomes aid in protein synthesis.
c. Ribosomes help protect the cell from its environment.
d. Ribosomes have enzymes that help with digestion.

50. The energy radiated by stars is produced by:

a. Neutronicity
b. Nuclear fusion
c. Nuclear fission
d. Gravitational confinement

51. The condition of balance and dynamic stability that characterizes living systems under normal conditions is called:

a. Homeostasis
b. Metabolism
c. Respiration
d. Symbiosis

Refer to the following for questions 52–53:

Your 9th grade biology class is about to take on its first animal dissection. You have already covered the procedure in detail during class, but you know that some of the students are still feeling nervous or even a little queasy.

52. What can you do to help make the dissection go more smoothly?

a. Remind them that medical students regularly dissect human cadavers, and that this is not really such a big deal
b. Set a timer for each section of the procedure, so the students stay on pace
c. Require each student write out their own step-by-step explanation of what they plan to do
d. Have the students speak out loud as they work, describing what they are doing

53. Which of the following procedures would be INCORRECT regarding dissection?

a. The specimen should be rinsed before handling.
b. Harmful chemicals should be disposed of according to district regulations.
c. Decaying specimens are never permitted.
d. Students with open sores on their hands that cannot be covered should be excused from the dissection.

54. If the moon is at the point in its cycle where it is between the earth and the sun, which moon phase would we observe from the earth?

a. New moon
b. Last moon
c. Full moon
d. First quarter moon

55. Which of the following creates a magnetic field?

a. The spinning and rotating of electrons in atoms
b. The separation of charged particles in atoms
c. The vibrational and translational motion of atoms
d. Loosely held valence electrons surrounding an atom

56. Which color of light has the highest frequency?

a. Blue
b. Red
c. Green
d. Violet

57. Which of the following blood components is involved in blood clotting?

a. Red blood cells
b. Platelets
c. Plasma proteins
d. Leukocytes

58. Conservative forces are forces that do not lose energy to processes like friction and radiation and where the total mechanical energy is conserved. Which statement best explains why the work done by a conservative force on an object does not depend on the path the object takes?

a. This is the definition of a conservative force.
b. The work done by the force of friction on an object depends on the distance the object moves.
c. Work can be positive, negative, or zero.
d. If a force is conservative, any component of the force is equal to the change in potential energy divided by the change in position.

59. In which of the following scenarios is work NOT applied to the object?

a. Mario moves a book from the floor to the top shelf.
b. A book drops off the shelf and falls to the floor.
c. Mario pushes a box of books across the room.
d. Mario balances a book on his head.

60. Earth's oceans have many little waves that are caused by the various wind speeds around the globe. However, one type of wave is caused by a celestial body. Which celestial body causes this wave?

a. Sun
b. Stars
c. Planets
d. Moon

61. Which of the following terms is NOT related to cell division in sexual reproduction?

a. Meiosis
b. Telophase
c. Fission
d. Prophase

62. Which of the following statements correctly compares rocks and minerals?

a. Minerals may contain traces of organic compounds, while rocks do not.
b. Rocks are classified by their formation and the minerals they contain, while minerals are classified by their chemical composition and physical properties.
c. Both rocks and minerals can be polymorphs.
d. Both rocks and minerals may contain mineraloids.

63. Remoras are fish that attach themselves to sharks and feed on the food particles left over by the larger fish. The shark is neither harmed nor helped by the remora's actions. This type of symbiotic relationship is best described as:

a. Parasitism
b. Commensalism
c. Mutualism
d. Passive transport

64. Which of the following body systems allows a person to move?

a. integumentary system
b. digestive system
c. endocrine system
d. muscular system

65. When we look at a straw in a glass of water, the straw appears broken or bent at the waterline. This appearance is a function of:

a. Scattering
b. Absorption
c. Reflection
d. Refraction

66. A ball is resting on the front end of a boat. The boat is moving straight forward toward a dock. According to Newton's first law of motion, when the front of the boat hits the dock, how will the ball's motion change with respect to the boat?

a. The ball will remain at rest.
b. The ball will move backward.
c. The ball will move forward.
d. The ball will move upward.

67. How are lipids different from other organic molecules?

a. They consist of repeating monomers to form long chains.
b. They are not water soluble.
c. They serve as catalysts.
d. Lipids store less energy per gram than carbohydrates or proteins.

68. Jim and John are working on their science fair project when they accidently break a beaker. What should the boys do?

a. Tell their teacher immediately
b. Clean up the broken glass themselves
c. Move away from the broken glass and continue working
d. Hide the broken glass so they don't get in trouble

69. Which of the following demographic changes would lead to a population with an older age composition?

a. Increased birth rate
b. Environmental pollution
c. Increased availability of food
d. Medical advancements that increase life expectancy

70. When you walk barefoot on a hot sidewalk, what process is primarily responsible for heat transfer from the sidewalk to your foot?

a. Conduction
b. Convection
c. Radiation
d. None of the above.

71. The best way to separate isotopes of the same element is to exploit:

a. Differences in chemical reactivity
b. Differences in reduction potential
c. Differences in toxicity
d. Differences in mass

72. Which of the following is a scalar quantity?

a. Acceleration
b. Velocity
c. Speed
d. Force

73. Students experimentally determine that the specific heat of copper is $0.410\ \frac{\text{J}}{\text{g}\cdot{}^{\circ}\text{C}}$. If the known value of the specific heat of copper is $0.385\ \frac{\text{J}}{\text{g}\cdot{}^{\circ}\text{C}}$, what is the percent error?

a. 6.10%
b. 16.4%
c. 6.49%
d. 15.4%

74. A space station is revolving in a circular orbit around Earth. Consider the following three statements:

I. The center of mass of the space station is necessarily located at its geometric center.
II. The center of mass is moving at a constant velocity.
III. The center of mass of the space station is moving at a constant speed.

Which of the following statements is true?

a. I is true.
b. II is true.
c. III is true.
d. I, II, and III are not true.

75. Which of the following materials has randomly aligned dipoles?

a. A non-magnetic substance
b. An electromagnet
c. A permanent magnet
d. A horseshoe magnet

76. For the reaction $CO_2(g) + H_2(g) \rightleftharpoons CO(g) + H_2O(l)$, which of the following will occur if the pressure of the reaction is increased?

a. The reaction order will increase.
b. The forward reaction rate will decrease.
c. The reaction equilibrium will shift to the right.
d. The reaction will stop.

77. The Earth's magnetic field protects it from:

a. Excess heat from the Sun
b. Radio waves from black holes
c. Solar wind
d. Impacts from space debris

78. Which of the following is an example of a density-dependent limiting factor?

a. Air pollution by a factory
b. The toxic effect of waste products
c. Nearby volcanic eruptions
d. Frosts

79. Any given temperature can be represented using three different temperature scales. Which temperature scale below yields a sequence of numbers from *lowest to highest* for the temperature of boiling water?

a. °C, °F, K
b. °F, °C, K
c. °F, K, °C
d. K, °C, °F
e. K, °F, °C

80. Which element will most likely form a covalently bonded compound when it bonds with sulfur?

a. Argon (Ar)
b. Iron (Fe)
c. Lithium (Li)
d. Oxygen (O)

81. Which of the following characteristics accurately describes authentic assessment techniques?

a. They are norm-referenced
b. They are designed to build higher-order thinking skills
c. They allow students to choose from a set of teacher-prepared responses
d. They measure students' performance at a specific point in time

82. Which of the following planets in our solar system is NOT a gas giant?

a. Saturn
b. Neptune
c. Venus
d. Jupiter

83. What are the numbers of neutrons, protons, and electrons in ^{238}U?

a. 238, 92, 238
b. 92, 146, 146
c. 146, 92, 92
d. 92, 92, 146

84. Which of the following correctly describes the image of a double concave lens?

a. Reduced, upright, virtual image
b. Enlarged, upright, virtual image
c. Reduced, inverted, virtual image
d. Reduced, upright, real image

85. What do all animals belonging to the Echinodermata phylum have in common?

a. They use multiple appendages for locomotion.
b. They use tube feet for locomotion and feeding.
c. They have an exoskeleton made of chitin.
d. They must shed their outer layer of skin to grow.

86. Which of the following is an example of a trace fossil?

a. A mouse jaw
b. A footprint
c. A shark tooth
d. A cast of a skull

87. What is the correct expression of $91,000 \times 87,000$ using scientific notation and significant figures?

a. 7.91×10^9
b. 7.9×10^9
c. 79.2×10^8
d. 79×10^8

88. Which statement is correct regarding the phenomenon of magnetism?

a. Opposite poles of magnets repel each other.
b. The like poles of magnets attract each other.
c. Magnets can attract/repel without touching.
d. Magnets work beyond their magnetic fields.

89. A normal human sperm must contain:

a. An X chromosome
b. A Y chromosome
c. 23 chromosomes
d. Both an X and a Y chromosome

90. Which of the following is a negative impact of reservoirs or dams?

a. Higher likelihood of flooding
b. Decreased dissolved oxygen
c. Increased rate of soil erosion
d. Less protection of water from pollution

91. Which of the following is the correct definition of a conductor?

a. A metal wire in an electrical circuit.
b. A material that contains movable electric charges.
c. A material that is not a semiconductor or insulator.
d. Any device that allows electricity to flow.

Refer to the following for questions 92–93:

A teacher in Arizona takes her class on a walk through a nearby park to study the flora and fauna of their local desert ecosystem. The students see cacti, snakes, and even evidence of coyote activity.

92. This activity is likely to appeal most to students who favor which learning style?

a. Visual
b. Auditory
c. Tactile
d. Kinesthetic

93. How should the teacher explain to students how these organisms are able to survive in harsh desert conditions?

a. Over thousands of years, these organisms have developed adaptations to survive in arid climates.
b. These organisms migrate out of the desert during the summer months, only living in the desert for a portion of the year.
c. Snakes, cacti, and coyotes work together to find sources of food and water.
d. Snakes, cacti, and coyotes are all aquatic species that live in ponds and rivers during the hot day.

94. Which statement best explains why the work done by a gravitational force on an object does not depend on the path the object takes?

a. Work depends on the path when there is friction. The longer the path, the more energy is required to overcome friction.
b. Gravitational fields that arise from the interaction between point masses always produce elliptical paths of motion.
c. A falling object experiences a change in potential energy.
d. When an object falls down, the work done by gravity is positive, and when an object is thrown up, the work done by gravity is negative.

95. What is the most common type of volcano on Earth?

a. Lava dome
b. Composite volcano
c. Shield volcano
d. Cinder cone

96. What are pure substances that consist of more than one type of atom?

a. Elements
b. Compounds
c. Molecules
d. Mixtures

97. All salts are made from a combination of what two types of substances?

a. A metal and a nonmetal
b. A nonmetal and an alkaline earth metal
c. A cation and an anion
d. A metal and a halogen

98. Which of the following molecules exhibits ionic bonding?

a. NaCl
b. CO_2
c. $C_6H_{12}O_6$
d. H_2O

99. A spoon that is placed in a bowl of hot soup becomes warm as a result of:

a. Convection
b. Conduction
c. Radiation
d. Advection

100. The process whereby a radioactive element releases energy slowly over a long period of time to lower its energy and become more stable is best described as which of the following?

a. Combustion
b. Fission
c. Fusion
d. Decay

101. A tropical flower is planted in a local garden. The garden is watered 2 to 3 times per week during all seasons. After only a few months, the tropical plant begins to droop and turn brown. How did environmental change most likely affect the tropical plant?

a. Being watered 2 to 3 times per week was not enough to sustain a tropical plant.
b. The new environment was too hot and burned the plant.
c. Insects attacked the plant causing it to wilt.
d. The new soil lacked the nutrients necessary to maintain the plant's health.

Refer to the following for question 102:

The fossilized remains of a bat have been found in volcanic rock dated to A.D. 79. Scientists studying the bat believe it to be an extinct species.

102. Which of the following statements is the best conclusion based on the data provided?

a. The volcanic eruption caused the extinction of this species of bat.
b. The only casualties from the eruption were bats.
c. The bat was probably from the same period as the volcanic eruption.
d. Bats never survive volcanic eruptions.

103. The structure of the Milky Way galaxy is best described as:

a. Spiral
b. Starburst
c. Elliptical
d. Irregular

104. Which of the following is true?

a. Materials whose atoms have strongly bound electrons conduct.
b. Materials whose atoms have loose electrons insulate electricity.
c. Materials with free electrons block the conduction of electricity.
d. Materials whose atoms feature tightly bound electrons insulate.

105. Which of the following conclusions can be drawn from the data presented in the graph below?

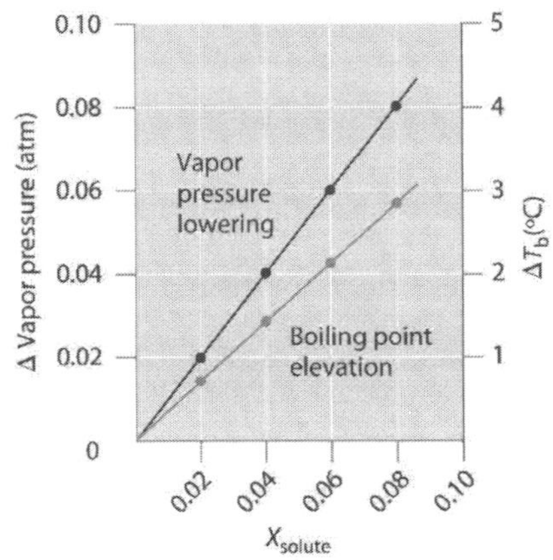

a. Increasing the solute increases the vapor pressure and decreases the boiling point of this solution.
b. Increasing the solute increases the vapor pressure and increases the boiling point of this solution.
c. Increasing the solute decreases the vapor pressure and decreases the boiling point of this solution.
d. Increasing the solute decreases the vapor pressure and increases the boiling point of this solution.

106. Plant A undergoes C4 photosynthesis. What type of environment would the plant most likely live in?

a. Plant A lives in a very cold environment.
b. Plant A lives in a very hot environment.
c. Plant A lives in a marine environment.
d. Plant A lives in a dark environment that lacks solar energy.

107. Which of the following is required for the activity of DNA polymerase?

a. Okazaki fragments
b. RNA primer
c. Single-strand binding protein
d. Leading strand

108. Which of the following processes is NOT part of the formation of sedimentary rock?

a. Layering
b. Cementation
c. Compaction
d. Heat

109. Between which two planets is the asteroid belt located?

a. Saturn and Uranus
b. Jupiter and Saturn
c. Earth and Mars
d. Mars and Jupiter

110. According to the laboratory safety rules, what should students be instructed to do first in case of a laboratory fire?

a. Notify the instructor
b. Locate the nearest exit
c. Use the fire extinguisher
d. Open the windows

111. What type of mutation is represented by the following sequence?

Original: 1 2 3 4 5 6
Mutated: 1 5 4 3 2 6

a. Breakage
b. Deletion
c. Insertion
d. Inversion

112. Cobalt-63 can be produced in a laboratory and is unstable. When it decays, a neutron in its core will likely decay into a proton, changing Cobalt-63 into Nickel-63. Which of the following products will be produced when a neutron decays into a proton?

I. alpha particles
II. beta particle
III. gamma particles

a. I only
b. III only
c. II and III
d. I, II and III

113. Which approach to assessment offers the strongest chance of quantifying what a student has learned?

a. Multiple choice tests
b. Essay questions
c. Combining several methods
d. Tests using a simple question-and-answer format

114. Genetic engineering:

a. Is a form of human reproduction
b. Always involves using restriction enzymes to cut DNA
c. Always involves transient expression of genes
d. Often involves using nucleases to cut DNA

115. Which of the following soil or rock types has a high porosity and a low permeability?

a. Sand
b. Granite
c. Gravel
d. Clay

116. A liquid is heated from 50 °C to 80 °C. Which of the following statements is generally true about the solubility of solids and gases in the liquid?

a. The solubility of solids will increase, and the solubility of gases will decrease.
b. The solubility of solids will decrease, and the solubility of gases will increase.
c. The solubility of solids will increase, and the solubility of gases will increase.
d. The solubility of solids will decrease, and the solubility of gases will decrease.

117. A student is working on a science project and is going through each step of the scientific method. After the student conducts his or her first experiment and records the results of the experimental test, what should the student do next?

a. Communicate the results.
b. Draw a conclusion.
c. Repeat the experiment.
d. Create a hypothesis.

118. Aerobic respiration in cells occurs in the _____.

a. cytoplasm
b. nucleus
c. mitochondria
d. cell membrane

119. Which of the following is the substrate for DNA ligase?

a. Okazaki fragments
b. RNA primer
c. Single-strand binding protein
d. Leading strand

120. A bacterial mini-chromosome used in recombinant DNA technology is called a

a. Centromere
b. Telomere
c. Plasmid
d. Transposon

121. This organelle contains digestive enzymes that break down food and unneeded substances. They are also thought to be linked to the aging process. What part of a cell does this describe?

a. Lysosomes
b. Chromatin
c. Plastids
d. Golgi apparatus

122. What is the name for the number of protons in an atom?

a. Mass number
b. Atomic mass
c. Molar mass
d. Atomic number

123. Which of the following divisions of plants produces seeds for reproduction?

a. Anthophyta
b. Lycophyta
c. Sphenophyta
d. Pterophyta

124. Which of the following statements about energy is false?

a. Mechanical energy is always conserved in an isolated system.
b. Total energy is always conserved in an isolated system.
c. Energy is never created or destroyed.
d. Matter can be transformed into energy

125. Which of the following kinds of plants is most likely to perform CAM photosynthesis?

a. Mosses
b. Grasses
c. Deciduous trees
d. Cacti

126. What type of chemical bond connects the oxygen and hydrogen atoms in a molecule of water?

a. Static bond
b. Aquatic bond
c. Ionic bond
d. Covalent bond

127. Electrons with greater amounts of energy are found _______ the nucleus than electrons with less energy.

a. closer to
b. farther from
c. more often inside
d. more randomly around

128. Which of the following statements regarding the principle of uniformitarianism is true?

a. Uniformitarianism is an argument for catastrophism.
b. Uniformitarianism is a key building block for Darwin's theory of evolution.
c. Uniformitarianism states that the past is the key to the present.
d. Uniformitarianism states that the fittest organisms will survive to reproduce.

129. A gas at constant volume is cooled. Which statement about the gas must be true?

a. The kinetic energy of the gas molecules has decreased.
b. The gas has condensed to a liquid.
c. The weight of the gas has decreased.
d. The density of the gas has increased.

130. Which of the following statements is true of Rocks (such as olivine) that are found at the top of Bowen's reaction series?

a. They are classified as metamorphic.
b. They weather more quickly than rocks found lower in the series.
c. They crystallize at lower temperatures than rocks found at the bottom of the series.
d. None of the above

131. According to Newton's law of universal gravitation, what happens to the force of attraction between two objects if the distance between them is doubled?

a. The force is reduced to one-half of the original amount.
b. The force is reduced to one-fourth of the original amount.
c. The force is quadrupled.
d. The force is doubled.

132. Which of the atomic models listed below is the most recent?

a. Rutherford's atomic model
b. Bohr's atomic model
c. Thomson's atomic model
d. Dalton's atomic model

133. Graham's law is best used to determine what relationship between two different materials?

a. Pressure and volume
b. Volume and temperature
c. Mass and diffusion rate
d. Diffusion rate and temperature

134. Hund's rule regarding electronic configuration states:

a. Electrons in the same orbital must have an opposite spin.
b. Electrons must fill lower energy orbitals before filling higher energy orbitals.
c. Electrons must populate empty orbitals of equal energy before filling occupied orbitals.
d. Electrons must have the same nuclear spin as the nucleus.

135. Tropical climate zones are characterized by:

a. Extreme temperature variations between night and day
b. Extreme temperature variations between seasons
c. Frequent rainfall
d. All of the above

136. Organized from high to low, the hierarchy of the human body's structure is as follows: organism, organ systems, organs, tissues. Which of the following comes next?

a. Molecules
b. Atoms
c. Cells
d. Muscle

137. During primary succession, which species would most likely be a pioneer species?

a. Lichens
b. Fir trees
c. Mosquitoes
d. Dragonflies

138. The reason for seasonal changes on earth is because of the earth's revolution around the sun and which unique aspect of the earth?

a. The earth rotates around the moon
b. The earth is tilted at its equator
c. The earth is tilted at its axis
d. None of these

139. Who proposed the quantum theory of light?

a. James Maxwell
b. Christiaan Huygens
c. Isaac Newton
d. Albert Einstein

140. Two cars driving in opposite directions collide. If you ignore friction and any other outside interactions, which of the following statements is always true?

a. The total momentum is conserved.
b. The sum of the potential and kinetic energy is conserved.
c. The total velocity of the cars is conserved.
d. The total impulse is conserved.

Answer Key and Explanations for Test #2

1. A: Quartzite, marble, and slate are all examples of metamorphic rocks, while granite is one of the most common types of igneous rocks.

2. D: Meiosis produces cells that are genetically different, having half the number of chromosomes of the parent cells. Mitosis produces cells that are genetically identical; daughter cells have the exact same number of chromosomes as parent cells. Mitosis is useful for repairing the body while meiosis is useful for sexual reproduction.

3. A: When light waves hit a convex lens, they are refracted and converge. A convex lens curves or bulges with the middle being thicker and the edges thinner. A magnifying glass is an example. Light rays are refracted by different amounts as they pass through the lens. After light rays pass through, they converge at a point called the focus. An object viewed with a magnifying glass looks bigger because the lens bends the rays inward. Choice B would indicate a concave lens as it would cause the light to be refracted and diverge. Light is not reflected in this case, so neither choice C nor D would be applicable.

4. C: Oxidation-reduction reactions occur inside dry cells, which are commonly called batteries. The cathode is the oxidizing agent because it accepts electrons from the anode. The anode is the reducing agent because it loses electrons.

5. B: Although like charges do repel, and unlike charges do attract, the question is indirectly asking about the law of conservation of charge. In other words, when someone mentions electric charge being conserved, they are saying the net charge of system remains constant. Charge originates from electrons and protons is only partially true because there are other elementary particles with charge. Charge can be created or destroyed because a photon will produce an electron-positron pair. There is also the example of a proton and electron combining to form a neutron.

6. D: Lower seed dispersal is not an advantage that angiosperms show over other types of plants. Gymnosperms, for example, have plentiful amounts of pollen, but it does not always hit its mark. Angiosperms are the most recently evolved plant division and contain at least 260,000 extant species. They are very diverse and occupy many habitats. Many other species in other plant divisions do not have true leaves. Gymnosperms have modified leaves in the form of needles. Double fertilization refers to how one sperm cell fuses with an ovule, forming the zygote. The second sperm forms into a triploid endosperm that provides energy for the embryo.

7. D: A lunar eclipse occurs when the full moon moves through the Earth's shadow. A solar eclipse occurs when a new moon passes between the Earth and the Sun.

8. D: Refer to the complete Punnett square in the explanation for question 10. Because male-pattern baldness is recessive, the offspring would need the *bb* gene combination in order to inherit this trait. Therefore, any offspring with the *B* gene will have a full head of hair. Possibilities 1, 2, and 3 all have the *B* gene.

9. D: The complete Punnett square is shown below.

	B	**b**
B	BB	Bb

b	Bb	bb

Because male-pattern baldness is a recessive gene, the offspring would need the *bb* gene combination in order to inherit this trait. Possibility 4 corresponds to the *bb* gene combination.

10. A: The large intestine's main function is the reabsorption of water into the body to form solid waste. It also allows for the absorption of vitamin K produced by microbes living inside the large intestine. The small intestine assists in some level of water reabsorption, but to a lesser extent than that of the large intestine.

11. C: One way to measure the density of an irregularly shaped object is to submerge it in water and measure the displacement. This is done by taking the mass (40 grams), then finding the volume by measuring how much water it displaces. Fill a graduated cylinder with water and record the amount. Put the object in the water and record the water level. Subtract the difference in water levels to get the amount of water displaced, which is also the volume of the object. In this case, 4.5 liters minus 2.5 liters equals 2 liters. Divide mass by volume (40 grams divided by 2 liters) to get 20 g/L (grams per liter).

12. A: A collision is considered elastic when neither object loses any kinetic energy. Since the cars latch together, this can't be the case. You could prove this by calculating the cars' kinetic energy: $KE = \frac{1}{2}mv^2$. If the railroad cars had bumpers instead of couplers, the moving car would stop and transfer all its momentum and kinetic energy to the stationary car, causing an elastic collision. In a closed system like this one, however, the conservation of momentum is an absolute law, where an object's momentum is its mass times its velocity. There are no external forces acting on the two cars. The only forces are between the two cars themselves. The momentum before the collision is the same as the momentum after the collision: $mv_{initial} + m\left(0\frac{\text{m}}{\text{s}}\right) = mv_{final} + mv_{final}$. So $mv_{initial} = 2mv_{final}$, and $v_{initial} = 2v_{final}$. Thus, the final velocity is half the initial velocity.

13. B: Phyletic gradualism is the view that evolution occurs at a more or less constant rate. Contrary to this view, punctuated equilibrium holds that evolutionary history consists of long periods of stasis punctuated by geologically short periods of evolution. This theory predicts that there will be few fossils revealing intermediate stages of evolution, whereas phyletic gradualism views the lack of intermediate-stage fossils as a deficit in the fossil record that will resolve when enough specimens are collected.

14. C: Overgrazing and deforestation directly contribute to soil erosion by destroying the natural ground cover that normally prevents soil from being washed and blown away. These activities can ultimately result in desertification, which renders land unsuitable for agriculture.

15. C: A physical change occurs when water condenses. The only thing formed during condensation is new intermolecular bonds. Therefore, no new covalent bonds form (B). The only time new atoms form is during a nuclear reaction (A). The water molecule is not ionizing, so no new ionic bonds form (D).

16. A: A formalized hypothesis written in the form of an if/then statement can then be tested. A statement may make a prediction or imply a cause/effect relationship, but that does not necessarily make it a good hypothesis. In this example, the student could rewrite the statement in the form of an if/then statement such as, "If the length of the string of the pendulum is varied, then the time it takes the ball to make one complete period changes." This hypothesis is testable, and doesn't simply make a prediction or a conclusion. The validity of the hypothesis can then be supported or disproved by experimentation and observation.

17. B: The ideal gas law $PV = nRT$ is rearranged to solve for V, and we get $V = \frac{nRT}{P}$. R is the gas constant, $\frac{0.08206 \text{ L atm}}{\text{mol K}}$, and the Celsius temperature must be converted to Kelvin, by adding 273 to 25 °C to obtain 298 K. The pressure must be converted to atmospheres, which 101 kPa is essentially 1 atm (0.9967 atm). Plugging the numbers into the equation we get $V = 1{,}000 \text{ mol} \times \frac{\left(\frac{0.08206 \text{ L atm}}{\text{mol K}}\right)(298 \text{ K})}{1 \text{ atm}}$, which gives $V = 24{,}453$ L. A liter is a cubic decimeter (dm^3) and when converted gives $V = 24.5 \text{ m}^3$.

18. A: A characteristic of a reputable scientific journal is that there is peer review of the quality of the research. The other choices may be characteristics of scientific journals, but these do not necessarily mean a journal is reputable.

19. B: The weight of the masses is determined from $W = mg$. In this case, there is a force to the left/down of $20 \text{ kg} \times 9.8 \text{ m/s}^2 = 196$ N, and a force to the right/down of $30 \text{ kg} \times 9.8 \text{ m/s}^2 = 294$ N. The net force is 98 N to the right/down. This force is moving both masses, however, which have a total mass of 50 kg. Using $F = ma$ and solving for acceleration gives $a = \frac{98 \text{ N}}{50 \text{ kg}} = 2 \text{ m/s}^2$.

20. A: A standing wave remains stationary, and the fixed points at both ends are the wave's nodes. Nevertheless, a standing wave with nodes at both ends of the string can have several forms. It may have one anti-node (i.e., it will arc across), two anti-nodes (this looks like a sine wave), three anti-nodes (with 1.5 sine waves), etc. However, waves with just one anti-node will have the longest wavelength and thus the smallest frequency. For a wave with one anti-node, the string will have only one-half of a wave, so 20 m represents a half-wavelength and the full wavelength is 40 m. Using the wave equation ($v = \lambda f$) gives the correct answer. $f = \frac{v}{\lambda} = \frac{4 \text{ m/s}}{40 \text{ m}} = 0.1$ Hz.

21. B: According to Gardner, naturalist intelligence is the ability to identify similarities, differences, and patterns in nature, natural life forms, and natural objects, e.g., rock types, mountain types, and animal and plant species. Kinesthetic, i.e., bodily-kinesthetic intelligence (A), is the ability for skillfully using one's body in controlled movements, e.g., sports, dance, etc. Logical-mathematical intelligence (C) is the ability for logical reasoning, e.g., in math problems, proofs, or scientific hypotheses. Spatial intelligence (D) is the ability to observe, reproduce, and discriminate among objects visually, and imagine and mentally manipulate visual images.

22. B: Approximately 96.5% of seawater is composed of hydrogen and oxygen. Although seawater does contain sodium, chlorine, magnesium, sulfur, and other dissolved solids, its primary components are the same substances that make up fresh water.

23. A: A ribosome is a structure of eukaryotic cells that makes proteins.

24. A: X-rays were put to clinical use within a month of their discovery, to image bone fractures and foreign objects in the body. Later they were used to locate tumors, and even later to fight cancer. Distant galaxies have been discovered by the detection of X-rays from stars. X-rays are commonly used as security scanners.

25. C: Both meiosis and mitosis occur in humans, other animals, and plants. Mitosis produces cells that are genetically identical, and meiosis produces cells that are genetically different. Only mitosis occurs asexually.

26. B: The compound $CuCl_2$ is an ionic compound consisting of Cu^{2+} ions and Cl^- ions. Ionic compounds are named from the cation and anion names. The name of this compound is copper (II) chloride. The Roman numeral II inside the parentheses indicates the oxidation state of copper ion.

27. B: Anthers produce microspores (the male gametophytes of flowering plants), which undergo meiosis to produce pollen grains.

28. D: In the image, the parts of the flower are as follows:

1. Ovary – the pollen-receiving portion of the flower that resides at the base of the pistil.
2. Anther – the pollen-bearing tip of the stamen.
3. Petal – The soft, colorful parts of the flower that attract pollinators and protect the inner parts.
4. Sepal – The outermost part of a flower that protect the developing bud before blooming.
5. Filament – The stalk that supports the anther.

Of the available choices, only choice D, the sepal, is not considered a reproductive organ of the flower.

29. B: When two crustal plates move apart, magma welling up could result in the formation of new crust. This has been shown to be occurring on the ocean floor where places of the crust are weaker. The crust spreads apart at these trenches, pushing outward and erupting at the ridges. When two crustal plates converge, sublimation occurs as one plate runs under another pushing it up. Two crustal plates sliding past one another is an example of a transform fault, which does not create new crust. A crustal plate being pushed down into the mantle does not form new crust but perhaps recycles the old one.

30. C: The pressure decreases to one-third. A gas in a closed container at constant temperature will decrease in pressure to one-third when the volume of the container is tripled. The ideal gas law is $PV = nRT$ where P is pressure, V is volume, n is the moles of the gas, R is the gas constant, and T is temperature. Dividing by volume gives the following expression for pressure:

$$P = \frac{nRT}{V}$$

Boyle's Law indicates that pressure and volume are inversely proportional. The pressure cannot be increased because that would imply that pressure and volume are directly proportional.

31. A: Newton's third law states that for every action there is an equal and opposite reaction. Put another way, if object A exerts a force on object B, then object B exerts a force of the same magnitude on object A in the opposite direction. Since we're considering the force of the box on the table to be the action force, the reaction force is then the force of the table on the box.

32. D: Trees absorb and use carbon dioxide to produce their own food. Humans breathe in oxygen and breathe out carbon dioxide. To a human, too much carbon dioxide is toxic and can cause serious problems. Plants use carbon dioxide and release oxygen as waste. This allows what is toxic to humans, carbon dioxide, to be used and transformed into breathable oxygen. A decrease in the number of trees decreases the amount of plants taking in carbon dioxide, causing the carbon dioxide levels in the atmosphere to rise.

33. A: The human body works best within a certain temperature range, around 98.6°F. When the body gets too cold or too hot it cannot function properly. The boy who is outside in the winter is cold. His body temperature is dropping below 98.6°F. His muscles start to contract causing him to shiver in order to generate heat. The girl is outside in the summer, and begins sweating to reduce her body temperature from rising too far above 98.6°F. In both cases, the children's bodies are trying to keep the temperature close to 98.6°F.

34. D: Water in the liquid state generally has a higher density than water in the solid state (ice). Unlike most other substances, which become progressively denser as they grow colder, water's density only increases until it reaches a maximum density around 4 °C, after which it begins to decrease as the temperature drops further.

35. C: All line segments on this graph represent acceleration since velocity divided by time equals acceleration. The line with the steepest slope represents the greatest acceleration. The steepest line is V, so option C is the correct answer.

36. D: Each time a cell divides, a few base pairs of DNA at the end of each chromosome are lost. Telomerase is an enzyme that uses a built-in template to add a short sequence of DNA over and over at the end of chromosomes—a sort of protective "cap". This prevents the loss of genetic material with each round of DNA replication.

37. D: The temperature of a substance during the time of any phase change remains the same. In this case, the phase change was from liquid to solid, or freezing. Latent heat of fusion, in this case, is energy that is released from the substance as it reforms its solid form. This energy will be released and the liquid will turn to solid before the temperature of the substance will decrease further. If the substance were changing from solid to liquid, the heat of fusion would be the amount of heat required to break apart the attractions between the molecules in the solid form to change to the liquid form. The latent heat of fusion is exactly the same quantity of energy for a substance for either melting or freezing. Depending on the process, this amount of heat would either be absorbed by the substance (melting) or released (freezing).

38. A: The rising and falling of the ocean's tides are directly influenced by the gravitational pull of the moon on the earth. High tide is found in areas closest and farthest from the moon because the moon pulls the water and earth toward it, leaving the water on the other side of the earth behind. Low tide occurs in the areas not affected by high tide. There are two tides each day.

39. C: The loss of biodiversity destabilizes ecosystems and impacts society by decreasing the food supply, decreasing the access to raw materials and clean water, and increasing the vulnerability to natural disasters.

40. B: Organisms that belong to the same taxonomic group of family are most alike. In biological taxonomy, the ranks in descending order are Domain, Kingdom, Phylum, Class, Order, Family, Genus, and Species. The ranks become more exclusive and specific as the classification descends. Phylum, class, and order are all higher than the family group. The higher the rank, the fewer requirements it takes to be a member. Two mnemonics for taxonomy are Dashing Kings Play Cards On Fat Green Stools or Dear King Philip Cuts Open Five Green Snakes.

41. D: *Binary fission* is the process of a bacterial cell splitting into two new cells. Fission is a form of asexual reproduction in which an organism divides into two components; each of these two parts will develop into a distinct organism. The two cells, known as daughter cells, are identical. *Mitosis*, on the other hand, is the part of eukaryotic cell division in which the cell nucleus divides. In *meiosis*, the homologous chromosomes in a diploid cell separate, reducing the number of chromosomes in each cell by half. In *replication*, a cell creates duplicate copies of DNA.

42. D: By allowing the students time to brainstorm where they feel the most bacteria can be found in their school, students can take ownership and become better engaged in the learning process. By discussing this in groups, the students can choose where they want to investigate, which should lead to further discussion and excitement in the groups about where they should test the bacteria. Allowing the students to brainstorm where to test does not help students determine what they still need to learn to conduct the experiment, since they may be unaware of what the teacher wants them to do after brainstorming is complete. While positive relationships may form in the group discussions, it is not the intended purpose of having the students brainstorm in groups for this activity. Group work is frequently a time when teachers can monitor their class and see which students understand the work they are performing; this is not necessarily the case in a group brainstorming session. Some students may be quieter than others while brainstorming but still understand the purpose of the assignment.

43. A: The center of an atom is known as the nucleus. It is composed of protons and neutrons. The nucleus is positively charged due to protons having a positive charge and neutrons being electrically neutral.

44. D: To make a buffer, a weak acid and its conjugate base or a weak base and its conjugate acid are commonly used. Buffers work by using the common-ion effect and result in little change in the pH when an acid or a base is added. HCl/NaOH is a strong acid/strong base combination and will not result in a buffer solution. Although the $HNO_3/NaNO_3$ and $H_2SO_4/NaHSO_4$ mixtures are conjugate acid/base pairs, both HNO_3 and H_2SO_4 are strong acids, not weak acids. Neither of these solutions would result in a buffer. Only the NaH_2PO_4/Na_2HPO_4 mixture would result in a buffer as it is a combination of a weak acid and its conjugate base.

45. D: It is true that the ocean's salinity is usually between 34 and 35 parts per thousand, or 200 parts per million. Oceans comprise about 70.8% of the Earth's surface, and the ocean's deepest point is over 10,000 meters below sea level. The Mediterranean is considered a sea, not an ocean.

46. C: Disruptive selection occurs when the environment favors alleles for extreme traits. In the example, seasonal changes can make different types of food available at different times of the year, favoring the large or small bills.

47. B: In a scientific lab, there are countless substances and tools that must be respected and used safely. Many chemicals and materials used in experiments can be very dangerous if not used properly and if students do not wear proper protective gear. Also, students should learn how to use sinks, hot plates, data collectors and other tools safely and efficiently. All of these lessons will allow students to interact properly with their environment and get the most out of their daily lessons and experiments.

48. C: In 2.4×10^4 years, 50% of the substance will have decayed. In another half-life, half of this will be gone, or 75%. 87.5% represents 3 half-lives, or a total of $3 \times 2.4 \times 10^4$ years = 7.2×10^4 years.

49. B: Ribosomes are organelles that help synthesize proteins within the cell. Cilia and flagella are responsible for cell movement. The cell membrane helps the cell maintain its shape and protects it from the environment. Lysosomes have digestive enzymes.

50. B: The energy radiated by stars is produced by nuclear fusion. This is the process whereby the nuclei of individual atoms bind together to form heavier elements and release energy outward. By the time this energy, which is created in the star's core, reaches the outer walls of the star, it exists in the form of light.

51. A: Homeostasis is the process whereby an organism maintains the constant internal conditions necessary for life. Dynamic equilibrium must be maintained even as external conditions continually change. Metabolism refers to the combined chemical processes within a living cell or organism that are necessary for maintaining life. Respiration refers to the process by which cells derive energy from organic molecules. Symbiosis refers to a close association of two dissimilar species that is usually beneficial to one or both of the organisms.

52. C: Having each student write out his own step-by-step instructions will help them visualize the process in their minds and make them feel more confident about what they are doing. During the actual lab session, the students will also find it helpful to have the procedure spelled out in their own words. Answer A will do little if anything to calm their nerves, and nothing to help them learn about the process. Answer B will likely only make the students more nervous and more likely to make mistakes, since they will feel rushed. Answer D is not a bad idea except that with so many people talking in one classroom, it may be a bit chaotic.

53. C: When performing a dissection in class, decaying specimens can be permitted under certain circumstances, but unknown specimens are never permitted. Rinsing the specimen before handling can help wash away excess preservative, which may be irritating. Disposing of harmful chemicals according to district regulations is always required. Excusing students with open sores on their hands that cannot be covered is a good precaution. Exposure to pathogens and toxic chemicals can occur through open breaks in the skin.

54. A: A new moon is one that is in between the earth and sun. The moon would then receive light on the side closest to the sun and its illuminated sides would not be directly visible to us on the earth.

55. A: A magnetic field is created by a spin magnetic dipole moment and the orbital magnetic dipole moment of the electrons in atoms. Therefore, it is the spinning and rotating of electrons in atoms that creates a magnetic field. The separation of charged particles in atoms describes the nucleus and electron clouds within an atom. The vibrational and translational motion of atoms creates thermal energy. Loosely held valence electrons surrounding an atom indicates a good electrical conductor.

56. D: The colors of the visible spectrum from the lowest to highest frequency are red, orange, yellow, green, blue, and violet. Therefore, violet has the highest frequency.

57. B: Platelets are cell fragments that are involved in blood clotting. Platelets provide a surface for the blood coagulation cascade. Its final steps are the formation of fibrinogen, which, when cleaved, forms fibrin, the "skeleton" of the blood clot.

58. D: Answers A, B, and C all shed light on what conservative forces are but do not answer the question of why the work on an object doesn't depend on its path. Friction is a force that causes kinetic energy to be lost and where the amount of loss depends on the path taken. Work can be expressed in multiple ways, including as the sum of potentials, and all that matters is the beginning and ending position. Think of this in terms of gravity, gravitational potential energy, and the work done by gravity. In this case, $W = \Delta PE = mg\Delta h$, where h is an object's height. Dividing work by the change in position shows $mg = \Delta PE/\Delta h$. Since mg is a force, you can say $F = \Delta PE/\Delta h$, or the force equals the work, or change in potential energy, divided by its change in position.

59. D: Mario balances a book on his head. In this example, work is not applied to the book because the book is not moving. One definition of work is a force acting on an object to cause displacement.

In this case, the book was not displaced by the force applied to it. Mario's head applied a vertical force to the book to keep it in the same position.

60. D: Although all of the answers are celestial bodies, natural bodies outside of the earth's atmosphere, only one influences the earth's tides. The moon's gravitational pull on the earth causes the seas to rise and fall as one large wave, known as a tide, with a very large wavelength as compared to waves formed by wind.

61. C: Fission, while it is a process of cell division, is a process within asexual reproduction. Meiosis (A) is the process of cell division in sexual reproduction. Prophase (D) is the second step of mitosis, while telophase (B) is the sixth phase of mitosis.

62. B: It is true that rocks are classified by their formation and the minerals they contain, while minerals are classified by their chemical composition and physical properties. Choice A is incorrect because rocks may contain traces of organic compounds. Choices C and D are incorrect because only minerals can be polymorphs and only rocks contain mineraloids.

63. B: Commensalism is a relationship between two organisms in which one organism is benefited and the other is neither harmed nor helped. Parasitism is a relationship in which one organism benefits but the other is harmed. Mutualism is a relationship in which both organisms benefit. Passive transport is a process such as osmosis by which materials are absorbed into cells.

64. D: The muscular system includes muscles, which allow a person's body to move. The integumentary system (A) includes organs such as the skin. While injuries to the skin can limit a person's range of movement, it does not enable movement. The digestive system (B) allows a person to eat and digest food, but does not allow a person to move. The endocrine system (C) is related to hormones, not a person's ability to move.

65. D: Refraction is the process whereby the speed of light is changed as it passes from one transparent medium, like air, to another, like water. The change in speed bends the light wave. Scattering (A) is the process whereby light bounces back at multiple angles when it strikes a rough or uneven surface (instead of bouncing back at a single angle as when it strikes a smooth surface). When light bounces back off a surface, this is reflection (C). Materials that do not reflect *any* light waves (smoothly or scattered) or refract any light waves appear opaque (i.e., we cannot see through them) because they take in all frequencies of light; this is absorption (B).

66. C: The ball will move forward with respect to the boat. Newton's first law of motion states that an object in motion tends to stay in motion until a force acts to change it. The ball is initially at rest with respect to the boat, but the boat is moving forward. When the front of the boat hits the dock, the boat quickly decelerates, but the ball does not. It continues to move forward because the force acting to stop the boat does not significantly affect the ball. With the ball now moving forward faster than the boat, the ball's motion relative to the boat is forward motion.

67. B: Unlike other organic molecules, lipids are not water soluble. They are largely nonpolar, and therefore hydrophobic. Lipids are not built from repeating monomers; this is characteristic of carbohydrates, proteins, and amino acids. Enzymes are proteins that can catalyze reactions. Lipids store more energy per gram than carbohydrates and proteins.

68. A: Anytime there is an accident in the lab, the first step is always to tell the teacher. Even if a student or students were doing something that they should not have been doing, such as horse playing in the lab, the teacher's first priority is still to make sure the students are safe. Telling the teacher will allow him or her to respond appropriately to the situation and make sure that all of the students remain safe.

69. D: Prolonging the life of individuals in a current population will lead to an older age composition. An increased birth rate will cause population growth, but a greater proportion will be younger, not older.

70. A: Heat between objects in contact with each other is transferred by conduction, choice A. Convection is transfer by currents within a body of fluid, and radiation is the transfer of heat between objects *not* in contact, through light rays emitted by the hotter object and absorbed by the cooler one.

71. D: Isotopes of the same element must have the same chemical behavior, and (A), (B), and (C) all represent, in one form or another, chemical behavior. Isotopes differ in mass, and this can be used to separate them by some appropriate physical property.

72. C: Vectors are quantities with both magnitude and direction. Scalars are quantities with magnitude but not direction. Since velocity, acceleration, and force have magnitude and direction, they are all vectors. Since speed only has magnitude, speed is a scalar.

73. C: Percent error is calculated by the following equation.

$$\text{Percent error} = \frac{\text{Experimental value} - \text{Theoretical value}}{\text{Theoretical value}} \times 100\%$$

$$\text{Percent error} = \frac{0.410 - 0.385}{0.385} \times 100\% = 6.49\%$$

The percent error for the students' specific heat of copper is 6.49%.

74. C: In a uniform gravitational field, such as occurs near Earth's surface, an object will move like a point mass located at the center of mass. However, this does not necessarily mean that the geometrical center of an object is the same as its center of mass, depending on its shape, design and mass distribution. The center of mass of a sphere or cube is at its geometric center because you can imagine the sphere as consisting of a large number of point masses located at certain points in space. Multiplying the point masses by their location and dividing by the total mass gives the center of mass. Statement I is not true because the space station may not be completely symmetrical. Statement III is true because the space station is undergoing uniform circular motion around Earth. If the orbit had been elliptical, this would not be true because the speed would have changed depending on the station's position. However, even though the speed is constant in a circular orbit, the velocity is not. Since velocity has a direction associated with it, and the space station is moving in a circular path, its velocity is constantly changing.

75. A: Magnetic poles occur in pairs known as magnetic dipoles. Individual atoms can be considered magnetic dipoles due to the spin and rotation of the electrons in the atoms. When the dipoles are aligned, the material is magnetic. Choices B, C, and D are all magnetic materials. Therefore, the magnetic dipoles in these materials are not randomly aligned. Only choice A has randomly aligned dipoles.

76. C: Because there are 2 moles of gas on the reactant side and 1 mole of gas on the product side, a pressure increase will increase the forward reaction rate force the reaction to go further to the right. This, in turn, lowers gas pressure to restore equilibrium. Reaction order is not affected by environment changes.

77. C: The Earth's magnetic field protects it from solar wind. Solar wind is a stream of highly charged radioactive particles that emanate from the Sun, and these particles are deflected by the magnetic field. The magnetic field is shaped like a bowl that covers the side of the Earth facing the Sun. It deflects most solar particles, but some are trapped in the Van Allen belt. Particularly strong bursts of solar wind allow particles to pass through this belt into the Earth's ionosphere and upper atmosphere, creating geomagnetic storms and auroras.

78. B: Density-dependent limiting factors on population growth are factors that vary with population density. Pollution from a factory, volcanic eruptions, frosts, and fires do not vary as a function of population size. Waste products, however, increase with population density and could limit further population increases.

79. A: The magnitude of the temperature on the Fahrenheit scale is calculated using the mathematical expression $°F = \frac{9}{5}°C + 32$. At the boiling point of water, 100 °C, the temperature in Fahrenheit is calculated to be 212 °F. Kelvin (absolute temperature) is calculated using the mathematical expression $K = °C + 273$. At 100 °C, the temperature in Kelvin is 373 K. Thus, the order from least to greatest is 100 °C, 212 °F, 373 K.

80. D: Covalent bonds form when two nonmetals bond. Oxygen (O) is the only nonmetal in the answer choices. Iron (Fe) is a transition metal. Lithium (Li) is an alkali metal. Argon (Ar) is a noble gas and does not react with other elements.

81. B: Authentic assessment techniques are designed to build higher-order thinking skills because they require students to construct their own answers instead of choosing from preselected answers. They also allow for the possibility that multiple "correct" answers are possible because students bring different perspectives and prior experiences to the material. They typically measure student performance over an extended period of time and are graded on a criterion-referenced basis (e.g., students are compared to an objective standard, rather than being directly compared to one another).

82. C: Venus is not a gas giant. The four gas giants are Jupiter, Saturn, Uranus, and Neptune. While these gas giants are larger than Earth and are composed mostly of gases, Venus is a terrestrial planet that is comparable in size to the Earth.

83. C: The mass number is the number of protons and the number of neutrons added together. The number of protons is also known as the atomic number and can be found on the periodic table; therefore, the number of neutrons is the mass number (238) less the number of protons (92), which equals 146 neutrons. The number of electrons always equals the number of protons in a neutral atom, so C is the correct answer.

84. A: A double concave lens is a diverging lens in which the light rays are spread apart. Therefore, the image formed by a double concave lens is always reduced, upright, and virtual regardless of the distance of the object from the lens.

85. B: Animals belonging to the phylum Echinodermata have tube feet for locomotion and feeding. About 7,000 species are extant in this phylum, including starfish and sand dollars. Tube feet are an organ system that provides locomotion, respiration, feeding, and sensory functions. Not all echinoderms have appendages. Having an exoskeleton made of chitin is characteristic of arthropods. Not all echinoderms shed their outer layer of skin to grow.

86. B: A trace fossil shows evidence of existence but is not an organism itself. A trace fossil can be contrasted with a body fossil, which has been formed from an organism. Other examples of trace fossils include eggs, nests, burrows, borings, and coprolites (fossilized feces). A mouse jaw and a shark tooth are examples of body fossils. A cast of a skull is a replica and neither a body nor a trace fossil.

87. B: Before taking significant figures into consideration, the product of 91,000 × 87,000 is 7,917,000,000. In scientific notation, the product is 7.917×10^9. Since each factor has two significant figures, the product should have two significant figures. The correct answer is 7.9×10^9.

88. C: Magnets do not have to be touching to attract or repel materials; they are able to do this from a distance. However, magnets do NOT work beyond their magnetic fields (D): the magnetic field is defined as the effective range or area of a magnet, so magnets only work within their magnetic fields by definition. Opposite poles of magnets do NOT repel (A), but instead attract each other. Conversely, the like poles of magnets do NOT attract (B), but instead repel one another.

89. C: As a haploid cell, normal human sperm must contain one chromosome of each of the 23 chromosome pairs. Twenty-two of these pairs are autosomal chromosomes, which do not play a role in determining gender. The remaining pair consists of either two X chromosomes in the case of a female, or of an X and a Y chromosome in the case of a male. Therefore, a normal sperm cell will contain 22 autosomal chromosomes and either an X or a Y chromosome—but not both—for a total of 23.

90. B: Water moves more slowly downstream of a dam. This results in less aeration and diffusion and lowers the dissolved oxygen content in the water.

91. B: Answer B correctly states the definition of a conductor. Answer C is incorrect because a current will also flow in an insulator, for example, although that current will be very low. In metals, the current flow caused by an electric field is much greater than in an insulator or semiconductor because the electrons are not bound to any particular atom, but are free to move. Answer D is incorrect because a vacuum tube is a device that electrons can flow in, but a vacuum tube is not considered a conductor.

92. D: Kinesthetic learners are most receptive to new information when they can use body movement to explore the world around them. Like tactile learners, they profit most from a hands-on approach to education. Visual learners learn best when they are shown pictures or written materials, while auditory learners absorb information most effectively when it is presented verbally.

While learning styles do vary some from person to person, all people do need learn from visual information, auditory information, and by hands-on learning. Different materials lend themselves to a different format, but where possible, the best practice when presenting information to others is to use a mixture of formats, including hands-on materials, visual, and auditory information to keep the materials engaging to all learners.

93. A: Many organisms, especially organisms that live in harsh conditions such as deserts or frozen icy areas, have developed specific adaptations that allow them to survive. For example, cacti are able to expand to store large amounts of water, coyotes absorb some water from their food, and snakes can escape the heat by hiding within rocks.

94. C: To determine how much work is done by a gravitational force, you should calculate the change in that object's potential energy $= \text{mgh}$, where $\text{m} = \text{mass}$, $\text{g} =$ the gravitational acceleration $9.8\ \text{m/s}^2$ and $\text{h} = \text{height}$. Therefore, the work done only depends on the change in height and not on the path taken. In answer A, the work done by gravity doesn't have anything to do with friction, so this is not a good explanation. Friction is a separate force. Answer D, although true, doesn't explain why the work doesn't depend on the path.

95. D: The cinder cone volcano is the most common type of volcano on Earth. A cinder cone has steep sides made of fallen cinders, which themselves are made of the lava that intermittently shoots into the air. A composite volcano, sometimes called the stratovolcano, has steep sides, so the explosions of ash, pumice, and silica are often accompanied by treacherous mudslides. Indeed, it is these mudslides that cause most of the damage associated with composite volcano eruptions. Krakatoa and Mount Saint Helens are examples of composite volcanoes. A lava dome is a round volcano that emits thick lava very slowly. A shield volcano, one example of which is Mt. Kilauea in Hawaii, emits a small amount of lava over an extended period of time. Shield volcanoes are not known for violent eruptions.

96. B: Elements and compounds are both pure substances. Elements consist of only one type of atom. Compounds consist of more than one type of atom. Molecules may make up either elements or compounds. Mixtures are two or more substances that are physically combined but not chemically united.

97. C: A salt is a neutral ionic compound consisting of a positively charged cation balanced with an equivalent amount of a negatively charged anion. Although it is very common for a salt to be composed of a metal and a nonmetal, this is not always true, as in the case of the salt ammonium acetate. The ammonium $(NH_4{}^+)$ and acetate (CH_3COO^-) ions are both polyatomic ions composed of only nonmetals. Likewise, many salts are composed of an alkali or alkaline earth metal and a halogen, but this is not always the case.

98. A: Sodium chloride exhibits ionic bonding due to the attraction between Na^+ ions and Cl^- ions. Typically, elements on the opposite sides of the periodic table (a metal and a nonmetal) form ionic bonds. Carbon dioxide, water, and glucose exhibit covalent bonding. Typically, elements on the same side of the periodic table (two or more nonmetals) form covalent bonds.

99. B: Conduction is the transfer and distribution of heat energy from one molecule to the next within a substance. The spoon becomes warmer because the heat from the soup is conducted along the spoon. Convection is the transfer of heat energy in a gas or liquid through the movement of currents. Radiation is the transfer of heat through empty space in the form of rays or waves. Advection is the transfer of heat or other atmospheric properties by the horizontal movement of air.

100. D: The process whereby a radioactive element releases energy slowly over a long period of time to lower its energy and become more stable is best described as decay. The nucleus undergoing decay, known as the parent nuclide, spontaneously releases energy most commonly through the emission of an alpha particle, a beta particle, or a gamma ray. The changed nucleus, called the daughter nuclide, is now more stable than the parent nuclide, although the daughter nuclide may undergo another decay to an even more stable nucleus. A decay chain is a series of decays of a radioactive element into different elements.

101. A: Tropical environments typically receive rain 5 to 6 times per week, even if it is only a brief afternoon shower. In its new environment, the tropical plant is not receiving enough water to survive.

102. C: If the bat was found in the lava from a volcanic eruption dated in 79 A.D., it is a reasonable conclusion that the bat came from that period.

103. A: The structure of the Milky Way galaxy is spiral, meaning it has curved "arms" stretching out from a central point. While spiral galaxies have a flat, disc-like appearance, elliptical galaxies are more three-dimensional and appear to be roughly the same shape regardless of the viewing angle.

104. D: When the electrons are strongly bound to the atoms of a substance, these atoms seldom release their electrons and thus do not conduct electricity well; such materials are electrical insulators (e.g., air, wood, glass, plastic, cotton, and ceramics). Metals and other substances whose atoms have free electrons that can separate from the atoms and move about are electrical conductors; electrical current flows freely through materials with loose electrons.

105. D: This graph shows the effect of increasing the amount of solute in a solution on both vapor pressure lowering and boiling point elevation. The change in vapor pressure is a decrease due to the label of *vapor pressure lowering*. As the amount of solute increases, the amount the vapor pressure is lowered continually increases. Increasing the solute decreases the vapor pressure. Increasing the solute also increases the amount the boiling point is elevated. Increasing the solute increases the boiling point of the solution.

106. B: Photosynthesis converts carbon dioxide into sugars that plants use. Three types of photosynthesis are C3, C4, and CAM. C3 is used by most plants. C4 plants live in areas with high temperatures and high light exposure. C4 first forms a four-carbon sugar instead of the three-carbon sugar formed by C3. Also, the stomata of C4 plants are faster at absorbing carbon dioxide and do not have to open as long, so less water is lost by transpiration. A C4 plant, such as saltbush, corn, or some grasses, would live in a very hot environment rather than a cold, marine, or dark environment. Plants that use the CAM (Crassulacean Acid Metabolism) type of photosynthesis also use water more efficiently as their stomata are closed during the day and open at night. Desert cacti are examples.

107. B: DNA replication begins with a short segment of RNA (not DNA). DNA polymerase cannot begin adding nucleotides without an existing piece of RNA (a primer).

108. D: The formation of sedimentary rock does not include heat. Of the three types of rock—igneous, sedimentary, and metamorphic—heat is essential to two: igneous and metamorphic. Sedimentary rocks are formed by sediments that get deposited and then compacted or cemented together. Sedimentary rocks are classified into detrital, organic, or chemical sediments. Answer A, layering, is correct since sediments can be deposited or otherwise formed in layers. Answer B, cementation, is also called lithification. Answer C, compaction, refers to the pressure forming sedimentary rock leading to cementation.

109. D: The main asteroid belt, which contains millions of asteroids, is between Mars and Jupiter.

110. A: Appropriate laboratory safety rules should include instructions to always notify the instructor in case of any emergency. In the case of a fire, the instructor should be notified first. Then appropriate measures can be taken to actually put out the fire.

111. D: An inversion mutation is represented in the sequence 1 5 4 3 2 6. An inversion error is a type of mutation where an entire sequence of DNA is reversed. In this case, 2 3 4 5 has been reversed to 5 4 3 2. Answer A, breakage, in a gene can mess up its function entirely or lead to a translocation of genetic information. Answer B, deletion, is when a section of DNA is omitted or lost. Answer C, insertion, is when an extra base pair is added to a DNA sequence. Deletions and insertions can lead to a frameshift effect where entire sequences are thrown off because one nucleotide is wrong. This could result in coding for the wrong amino acid and non-functioning proteins.

112. C: Cobalt-63 has too many neutrons to be stable. By emitting a beta particle (aka an electron) one of the neutrons in the cobalt is converted to a proton, thereby maintaining the mass number but changing the atomic number from 27 (cobalt) to 28 (nickel). In addition, some energy is radiated away in the form of gamma particles. Electron emission is usually associated with the emission of gamma rays because the daughter nucleus is not likely to be in a ground state. The daughter nucleus, in other words, is likely to be unstable and emit a gamma ray.

113. C: Some students perform better on tests, while others do better with papers or other projects. Just as students learn in a variety of ways, their talents for expressing what they have learned also varies widely. A teacher that evaluates students based on a wide variety of tasks will come away with a much more complete picture of each student's strengths and weaknesses.

114. D: *Genetic engineering* is a general term to describe altering DNA sequences through adding or removing pieces of DNA from a native sequence. In the earliest genetic engineering processes, restriction enzymes were used to perform this "clipping" function, but other methods have been devised and are in use today. Current technologies include those using nucleases (such as CRISPR-Cas9, zinc-finger nucleases, or TALENs) or site-specific recombinases.

115. D: Porosity is a measure of how much water the soil can retain. Permeability is a measure of how easily water can travel through that soil. Clay has a high porosity because it holds a lot of water. Clay has a low permeability. Since it is fine-grained, water flows very slowly through it. Sand and gravel have high porosities and high permeabilities. Granite has a low porosity and a low permeability.

116. A: The higher the temperature of the liquid, the greater the solubility of the solid, while the higher the temperature, the lower the solubility of the gas.

117. C: Repeating the experiment validates data. Each separate experiment is called a repetition. It should be possible to replicate the results of experiments or tests. Similar data gathered from many experiments can also be used to quantify the validity of the hypothesis. Repeating the experiments allows the student to observe variation in the results. Variation in data can be caused by a variety of errors or may be evidence against the hypothesis. Answer D, create a hypothesis, comes before experiments. Answer A, communicate the results, and B, draw a conclusion, occur after testing.

118. C: The aerobic respiration process has four steps. The first step, glycolysis, occurs in the cytoplasm. The second through fourth steps (the formation of acetyl coenzyme A, the citric acid cycle, and the electric transport chain and chemosmosis) occur in the mitochondria. Mitochondria are the cells' power producers. They create energy for cellular functions and processes, such as aerobic respiration, which involves the oxidation of glucose molecules.

119. A: DNA synthesis on the lagging strand forms short segments called Okazaki fragments. Because DNA polymerase can only add nucleotides in the $5' \rightarrow 3'$ direction, lagging strand synthesis is discontinuous. The final product is formed when DNA ligase joins Okazaki fragments together.

120. C: Plasmids are small circular pieces of DNA found in bacteria. Plasmids are widely used in recombinant DNA technology. They are cut with restriction enzymes and DNA of interest is ligated to them. They can then easily be used to transform bacteria.

121. A: A lysosome is an organelle that is thought to be linked to the aging process and contains digestive enzymes that break down food and unneeded substances. Chromatin is the structure created by DNA and various proteins in the cell's nucleus during interphase and condenses to form chromosomes. Plastids are found in plants and algae. They often contain pigments and usually help make chemical compounds for the plant. The Golgi apparatus prepares macromolecules like proteins and lipids for transport.

122. D: The number of protons in an atom is the atomic number. Protons are the fundamental positive unit of an atom. They are located in the nucleus. In a neutral atom (an atom with neither positive nor negative charge), the number of protons in the nucleus is equal to the number of electrons orbiting the nucleus. Mass number is the number of nucleons (particles in the nucleus) of a particular isotope. Atomic mass is the average mass of the various isotopes of a given element. Molar mass is the mass of 1 mole of a substance.

123. A: Anthophyta is a division of plants that produces seeds as part of reproduction. Spermatopyta is the broader group that includes all plants that produce seeds for reproduction, which includes gymnosperms and angiosperms (the same group as anthophyta). Anthophyta are also known as the group that contains flowering plants. It is the largest and most diverse grouping of plants and includes many food, clothing, and medicinal uses for humans. Grains, beans, nuts, fruits, vegetables, spices, tea, coffee, chocolate, cotton, linen, and aspirin are all derived from plants from anthophyta. Lycophyta is a small group of plants including club mosses and scale trees. Sphenophyta contains about thirty species including horsetails, foxtails, or scouring rushes. Pterophyta contains non-seed plants like ferns. Lycophyta, sphenophyta, and pterophyta all use spores to reproduce sexually.

124. A: The total energy of an isolated system is always conserved. However, the mechanical energy may not be, since some mechanical energy could be converted into radiation (light) or heat (through friction). According to Einstein's famous equation $E = mc^2$, where E is energy, m is mass, and c is the speed of light, energy can be converted into mass, and vice versa (like in nuclear reactions). This does not affect the conservation of energy law, however, since the mass is considered to have an energy equivalent. This equation does not tell anything about the mechanical energy of a particle; it just shows how much energy would be generated if the mass was converted directly into energy.

125. D: Crassulacean acid metabolism (CAM) photosynthesis occurs in plants that grow where water loss must be minimized, such as cacti. These plants open their stomata and fix CO_2 at night. During the day, stomata are closed, reducing water loss. Thus, photosynthesis can proceed without water loss.

126. D: A covalent bond is one in which atoms share valence electrons. Within a water molecule, one oxygen atom and two hydrogen atoms share valence electrons to yield the H_2O structure.

127. B: Electrons with greater amounts of energy are found farther from the nucleus than electrons with less energy. The principal quantum number describes the level or shell that an electron is in. The lower the number, the closer the electron is to the nucleus and the lower it is in energy.

128. B: Darwin studied Lyell's work *Principles of Geology* while sailing around South America and the Galapagos Islands. Lyell's theory of uniformitarianism supposes that all things are continuing in the same uniform natural processes and that the changes to the Earth's crust have arisen from these continuous, uniform processes. Darwin was inspired by this theory and used it as a foundation for his theory of evolution, adopting the phrase that "the present is the key to the past" to the evolutionary history of life on Earth. Choice C is incorrect because it reverses the phrase. Choice A is incorrect because uniformitarianism is completely opposed to the idea of catastrophism, which argues that the majority of Earth's features are a result of violent, sudden events, such as meteorites and other natural disasters. Finally, D is incorrect because natural selection states that the fittest organisms will survive to reproduce.

129. A: The kinetic energy of the gas molecules is directly proportional to the temperature. If the temperature decreases, so does the molecular motion. A decrease in temperature will not necessarily mean a gas condenses to a liquid. Neither the mass nor the density is impacted, as no material was added or removed, and the volume remained the same.

130. B: Rocks (such as olivine) that are found at the top of Bowen's reaction series weather more quickly than rocks found lower in the series. This is because rocks high in the series crystallize at higher temperatures than those found lower in the series. This means they are less stable and more susceptible to weathering than rocks that crystallize at lower temperatures, such as quartz.

131. B: According to the law of universal gravitation, the force of attraction between two objects is inversely proportional to the square of the distance between the two objects. If the distance increases, the force decreases. If the distance is doubled, the force is reduced to one-fourth of the original amount.

132. B: Dalton stated that atoms are hard spheres. Thomson proposed the plum pudding model, in which electrons are embedded in a sphere of positive charge. Rutherford introduced the planetary model, in which electrons circularly orbit a small central nucleus. Bohr's model stated that electrons move in regions of space called orbits. This would later be expanded to "orbitals" of the later quantum-mechanical model.

133. C: Graham's law of diffusion allows one to calculate the relative diffusion rate between two different gases based on their masses.

134. C: Hund's rule states that electrons must populate empty orbitals of similar energy before pairing up. The Aufbau principle states that electrons must fill lower energy orbitals before filling higher energy orbitals. The Pauli Exclusion Principle states that no two electrons in the same atom can have the same four quantum numbers, and, therefore, two electrons in the same orbital will have opposite spins.

135. C: Tropical climate zones are characterized by frequent rainfall, especially during the monsoon season, and by moderate temperatures that vary little from season to season or between night and day. Tropical zones do experience frequent rainfall, which leads to abundant vegetation.

136. C: Cells come after tissues and are followed by molecules and then atoms at the very bottom of the hierarchy. Muscle tissue is a type of tissue, so muscles do not have a separate place in the hierarchy but instead fall within the types of tissues.

137. A: Pioneer species colonize vacant habitats, and the first such species in a habitat demonstrate primary succession. Succession on rock or lava often begins with lichens. Lichens need very little organic material and can erode rock into soil to provide a growth substrate for other organisms.

138. C: The earth experiences seasons because it revolves around the sun while tilted on its axis, exposing one hemisphere to the sun more than the other hemisphere. The hemisphere closest to the sun will be experiencing summer, while the other hemisphere has winter. The Northern Hemisphere and Southern Hemisphere experience opposite seasons all year long.

139. D: Isaac Newton proposed the particle or corpuscular theory of light. Huygens proposed the wave theory of light. Maxwell showed that light can be modeled as an electromagnetic wave. Einstein described electromagnetic radiation as bundles of energy proportional to frequency in the quantum theory of light.

140. A: In a closed system (when you ignore outside interactions), the total momentum is constant and conserved. The total energy would also be conserved, although not the sum of the potential and kinetic energy. Some of the energy from the collision would be turned into thermal energy (heat) for example. Nor is the total velocity conserved, even though the velocity is a component of the momentum, since the momentum also depends on the mass of the cars. The impulse is a force over time that causes the momentum of a body to change. It doesn't make sense to think of impulse as conserved, since it's not necessarily constant throughout a collision.